Step by Step Guide to
EASY ICING

Marguerite Patten

HAMLYN

London · New York · Sydney · Toronto

Contents

Acknowledgements

The author and publishers gratefully
acknowledge the help received from the
following firms who have kindly provided
the colour pictures as listed below:

The Australian Gas Light Co.
Christmas cake *page* 55 with plastic icing (top)

Kake Brand
Birthday cake *page* 63

Nestlé Company
Coffee cream roll *page* 31

Stork Cookery Service
Chocolate layer cake *page* 19
Crystal cake *page* 27
Christmas cake *page* 55 (bottom)

Syndication International
Christening cake *page* 59
American chocolate layer cake *page* 31
Assorted small cakes *page* 23
Wedding cake *page* 51

The birthday cake shown on the jacket was
coated with white plastic icing and the
delicate flowers moulded from pink plastic
icing: also shown are Butterfly cakes and
Cherry buns. (Photograph by John Lee.)

Published by
The Hamlyn Publishing Group Limited
London · New York · Sydney · Toronto
Hamlyn House, Feltham, Middlesex, England
© The Hamlyn Publishing Group Limited 1972

First Published 1972
Second Impression 1973

ISBN 0 600 33059 1·

Printed in Spain by Mateu-Cromo
Artes Gráficas, S.A., Madrid

Introduction

I have greatly enjoyed compiling this book of Easy Icing, for there is a great sense of achievement in producing really professional-looking iced cakes, biscuits and desserts. Not only do they *look* good, but will *taste* good too, if a well balanced recipe is followed.

Do not be impatient, though, learning to ice cakes, etc., takes time and practice. So I have first dealt with simple icings that are attractive to look at, delicious to taste, but not difficult to make.

Successful icing depends upon:

a) choosing the right type of icing for each type of cake. Page 8 onwards describes this in detail; remember some icings are ideal for light sponge cakes, but quite wrong for a rich fruit cake which needs time to mature.

b) taking the trouble to make your icing just the right consistency; if too stiff it is difficult to handle, and if too soft it does not hold its shape.

c) using the right equipment. Many icings can be spread neatly with an ordinary palette knife; it is only when you wish to pipe, or make flowers, etc., that you require pipes and icing nails, as described on page 50.

d) following instructions carefully. Where recipes specify *sieved* icing sugar it is essential to use this; other recipes do not demand this, and it means you can expect any small lumps to come out when the sugar is mixed with liquid (unless the icing sugar is very lumpy, due to damp storage conditions).

e) choosing the best quality flavouring you can afford.

Each recipe in this book gives an appropriate time for storage. This does not mean the icing will 'go bad' if kept longer, for icings do not spoil like ordinary cooked or raw food, due to the high percentage of sugar used. It simply means that after this period you may be disappointed in either the appearance or taste of the icing. For example, water or glacé icing begins to crack after a day or so, while Royal icing keeps a very long time but tends to become over-hard. I have also given storage times for the cakes in this book; if you wish to vary the suggested filling or topping you can, therefore, select those with the same 'length of life'.

I hope you find the step-by-step illustrations helpful, and I would like to record my thanks to the many people who have assisted in preparing these.

Marguerite Patten

Easy toppings for cakes

This is a book about icing and iced cakes; but a cake can be made to look extremely interesting with simple toppings, apart from icing. On page 20 are a selection of toppings that are baked with the cakes.

One of the simplest unbaked decorations is just to dust the top of a cooked cake or sponge with sieved icing sugar, or castor sugar. This can be made more interesting if the sugar (in this case icing sugar is better) is shaken over a doily as 1 below.

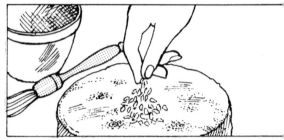

1 Choose a doily with a fairly clear-cut design. Put this on top of the cake. It is important that the cake is quite flat on top so the doily fits well. Shake the sieved icing sugar over this, then lift the doily up very carefully. The design in icing sugar is then left on the cake.

2 *Jam and coconut coating.* Brush the top of a large cake with warmed sieved jam or warmed jelly (apricot or rasberry jams are ideal). Sprinkle with desiccated coconut, then decorate with halved glacé cherries and leaves of angelica. Brush the under-side of these with a little jam or jelly so that they 'stick' to the coconut.

3 *Jam and nut coating.* Prepare the top of the cake as stage 2 above. If you wish to coat the sides of the cake as well, do this first as shown on page 6, then coat the top of the cake. Press chopped walnuts, or blanched almonds, over the cake in place of coconut. Decorate with whole blanched almonds that are browned under the grill, or halved walnuts. To coat small cakes see page 25.

4 *Cream and chocolate coating.* Top a cake with whipped cream or mock cream, page 66, then grate chocolate over the top. Use the coarse side of the grater.

Icing tools you need

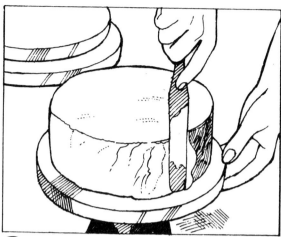

1 Basic tools are those things that are doubtless already in use — these are quite adequate for simple icings: a) a basin or mixing bowl; b) a sieve; c) a wooden spoon; d) a palette knife; e) a wire cooling tray (used to cool cakes); f) scales to ensure correct weights; g) a rolling pin and sugar dredger, for marzipan and other icings that need rolling out.

2 It is worthwhile adding a turn-table as you become more experienced in icing. It enables you to place the cake (on its board) on the turn-table, then to revolve this as you coat and pipe the cake. It means you never stretch across the cake and risk smudging the icing. An upturned basin is a simple substitute. Also shown in the picture are cake boards, upon which to put the cake before icing.

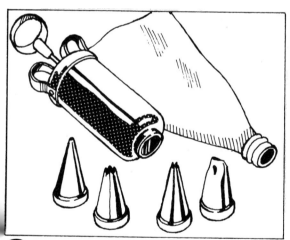

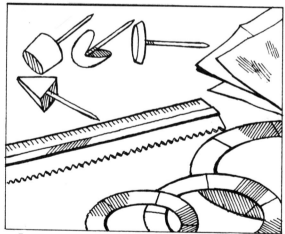

3 If you plan simple piping, then you need a piping bag, either nylon or paper — shown a) the nylon bag has a screw attachment for the various pipes. If preferred, buy an icing syringe b) — many people find this less easy to use. In the front of the picture are the most useful pipes for the start of a collection — writing pipes; a star; a rose pipe; a pipe that gives a rope design, which makes an edging.

4 These tools are important to produce more ambitiously iced cakes: a) icing nails, to make flowers, trellis, etc., see pages 48 to 52, you also need a little waxed paper; b) icing rings enable you to plan an accurate design on the cake; c) shows the long plastic ruler, one side giving a plain edge the other a serrated edge, this is very useful for large cakes.

Making icing

Each basic recipe outlines the essential stages, but most recipes for icing mention the following:

1 SIEVING . . . this is done to remove all lumps from icing sugar. Use a fine-meshed sieve and push the icing sugar through into a large bowl or basin. A wooden spoon does this most efficiently. Make sure the sieve fits into the basin or bowl so that no icing sugar is wasted round the edges.

2 BEATING . . . this gives the right consistency, binds the various ingredients together, and helps to give a good colour to Royal icing. This can be done by hand or with an electric mixer. Each recipe gives hints on using the mixer correctly.

3 COATING . . . this can mean either covering the top, or top and sides, with icing. Each icing recipe gives any special hints needed for doing this. The most important point is to try and put all the icing on the cake, THEN spread carefully; rather than coat a small area, then add more icing and coat another small area, etc.

4 COATING WITH NUTS, ETC . . . when the cake has been coated with icing or jam it is often rolled in nuts or coconut. To coat the sides hold the cake rather like a 'hoop'. Place the chopped nuts or coconut on a sheet or wide strip of greaseproof paper and roll the cake slowly along the paper so that it 'picks up' a coating.

5 PIPING . . . means forcing icing through a bag (page 48 describes these) or syringe, and an icing pipe, which gives the correct design. Not all icings are suitable for piping, see page 52. If you wish a flowing design, etc., hold the pipe at the angle shown. For an upright rosette, star, etc., hold the pipe above the cake, see page 48.

6 MOULDING . . . means handling the icing to form flowers, etc. This is not difficult to do, but you must use the correct type of icing, and spend time 'working' it, until it becomes soft and pliable, see pages 56, 57.

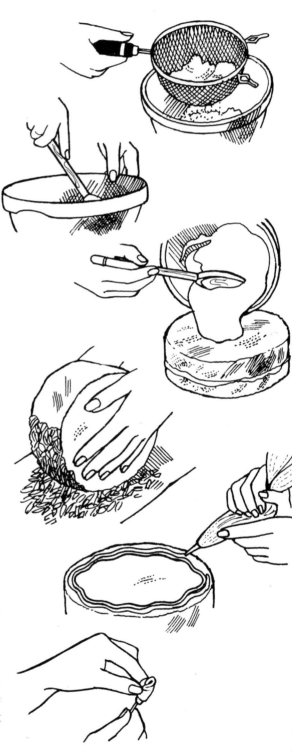

Making cakes

There are a variety of ways in which one can make cakes, etc., this book includes all of these — the basic techniques are:

1 RUBBING IN . . . this means rubbing some kind of fat into the flour, and is generally used for the plainer types of cakes, pastry and biscuits. Use the tips of your fingers (so the mixture does not become sticky) and allow the mixture to drop back into the bowl; it should look like fine breadcrumbs.

2 MELTING . . . this means allowing the fat, often with sugar and golden syrup, to heat in a pan until the fat has melted. It is then poured on to the flour, etc., and the mixture beaten until smooth. Gingerbreads and rather moist cakes are made by this method.

3 BEATING . . . this is mentioned in the melting method, described above, but is also used to blend the ingredients in many cakes. This vigorous movement can spoil the texture of light cakes, such as a sponge. Over-beating of rich fruit cakes is not advisable. Use a wooden spoon for hand beating, or medium speed with the mixer.

4 CREAMING . . . this is where the fat and sugar are beaten together until soft and light, then the rest of the ingredients blended with this mixture. This method is used for many cakes. Cream with a wooden spoon, or medium speed with the mixer. Do not melt the fat; this stops air being incorporated into the mixture.

5 WHISKING . . . this is used for a very light sponge. The eggs and sugar are whisked until like thick cream, then the other ingredients added. Whisking is also used for meringues, see page 75. It is essential to use some kind of egg whisk to give the light texture, or a high speed on the mixer.

6 FOLDING . . . this is referred to in a number of cake recipes. It means that the ingredients (generally flour or sugar) should be added very gently and carefully so that the light texture is not lost.

Choosing Icings

Mention has been made of the wise choice of icing in the introduction: let me explain a little more fully.

SIMPLE ICINGS

Glacé icing

The simplest icing of all is a water icing, or, as it is more often called, a glacé icing. This is made by blending icing sugar and water, or water and flavouring, or fruit juice, to give a consistency that can be spread very easily. The icing dries quickly and because it is soft and flowing can be spread over light, and often delicate, sponges without fear of spoiling them. The disadvantage of a glacé icing is that it often cracks after a few days, so it is not wise to use this on cakes that are to be kept for any length of time. If used on biscuits that are to be stored it can make them soft (due to the high water content) so it is advisable to spread the icing on the biscuits the day they are to be eaten. For details see pages 74 and 77. You cannot use glacé icing for piping, as it does not hold shapes.

Butter icing

Butter icing should be a combination of butter, icing sugar and flavouring. Today the very excellent margarines and cooking fats are often used as a basis. This icing can be used to coat a cake, as a filling, or for piping. In fact I always feel it is the best icing to use when you begin to learn about piping. Recipes vary slightly; some use a higher percentage of icing sugar than others — this produces a harder texture. Butter icing keeps for some time, unless the weather is very hot. The disadvantages of butter icing are that it does not give a 'shiny' look on cakes (as glacé or Royal icings) and it never becomes sufficiently hard to be used on wedding cakes under pillars, for it could not support the weight of these.

Marzipan

Although there *is* a marzipan or almond paste made by boiling sugar and water (as in a fondant) then combining these with ground almonds, this is used rarely at home.

The most popular marzipan is made by blending ground almonds with icing and castor sugars, egg and flavouring. This can be varied, see page 39. Marzipan is a very versatile icing; it can be used under other icings, as a covering itself, and for moulding into flowers if wished. It keeps for a very considerable time.

Careful handling is very important with marzipan, and this is explained more fully on page 38. Over-handling makes it become 'oily' and this can spoil the appearance of the top icing. Although marzipan is used as an 'undercoat' for cakes it can also be used as the top coat, the best known examples being Battenburg cake and Simnel cake, pages 42 and 39. If softened slightly it can be used as a filling, page 29, and the basis for petits-fours, see page 77.

Fresh cream

This may not be considered a true icing, but I have included it as it is used so often as a filling and as a topping for light sponge cakes, gâteaux, etc. If whipped *correctly*, i.e. not over-whipped so that it becomes curdled, it is excellent for piping. Fresh cream may be sweetened and flavoured; it is then often called Crème Chantilly. The disadvantage of cream is that is becomes sour quickly, so you cannot use it on a cake you wish to keep — unless stored in a home freezer.

Royal icing

I have included this under simple icings for it is easy to make, although it needs considerable beating and careful handling. Royal icing is ideal for coating wedding cakes, etc., and for the most intricate piping. Perhaps the greatest disadvantage is that it can become too hard — although one can adjust the texture — but it is not a versatile icing, for it cannot be put on to soft textured cakes, see page 44.

ESS SIMPLE ICINGS

American frosting

Frosting is only difficult in that the sugar and water mixture must be boiled to the correct temperature, in order that the icing will 'set' properly. Full details on page 36. This icing is very adaptable. Although it sets firmly (but never becomes over-hard) on the outside, it is sufficiently soft – if used as a filling – to be put into delicate sponge-type cakes. On the other hand, it can be used instead of Royal icing for Christmas cakes. One can coat the cake without using marzipan underneath. It keeps well for a long period.

Frosting like this cannot be used for piping; the only other disadvantage is that it sets very quickly, so that quick handling is essential.

Fondant icing

Fondant is another 'boiled' icing. It can be rolled out to coat a cake, if wished, and also for moulding flowers, etc. A large quantity can be made at one time, then stored, ready to be used at a later date. The icing can be used to coat light cakes, as a substitute for marzipan, and on fruit cakes, with or without marzipan. The disadvantage, if any, is that, like American frosting, you must be sure that the sugar syrup reaches the correct temperature. Although page 36 gives simple ways of testing when boiled icings are ready, if you use fondant (or other boiled icings) a great deal, a sugar thermometer would be a wise investment. Fondant icing cannot be used for piping.

Fudge icing

This icing, like fudge in flavour but soft enough to spread over a cake as a coating and to use as a filling too, has limited use, since it only combines well with certain cakes. It is worth making, as the combination of the delicate sponge and thick fudge layers is delicious. It blends best with coffee and chocolate cakes, see page 68. Fudge icing is at its best when freshly made; it hardens with keeping.

Plastic icing

This is another type of fondant icing but does not need cooking, and it is a speciality in Australia, where it is used to coat all rich cakes, as an alternative to Royal icing. It is mixed, moulded, then rolled out, rather like marzipan, and put over the cake. It can be used with or without marzipan. The art is to rub it gently and firmly with icing sugar on the palm of your hands, until it shines like satin, see page 53. As a moulding icing it is splendid, too, so that flowers, etc., may be made to look as delicate as real ones. It never becomes as hard as Royal icing, but can be kept for a considerable time. The only disadvantage is that some people do not like the flavour as much as that of Royal icing.

Chocolate

Many people find it quite difficult to melt chocolate to retain texture and shine. Page 43 gives details. Chocolate can be used for decoration, and to add to fillings.

Vanilla cream

Often called Confectioner's Custard, this filling is an ideal alternative to real cream. It is not used as an icing, but can be put into pastries, cakes, etc. It is not difficult to make, but takes time and care to blend the ingredients well. It keeps a little longer than real cream, but is still highly perishable, see page 66.

Mock cream

The recipe on page 66 is a good alternative to real cream. It is cheaper and can be used as a filling, covering, and, if well made, for piping too. It keeps a little longer than fresh cream.

Jam glaze

Use to coat cakes *under icings*, so crumbs do not spoil these, also as a glaze, see page 67.

Using glacé icing

1 Put 8 oz. icing sugar and water, see below, into either a saucepan or basin. There is no need to sieve the sugar unless very lumpy. Either stir over a gentle heat until well blended, or mix in the basin. A mixer is hardly necessary.
For stiff consistency: use ¾–1 tablespoon water, see stage 3.
For flowing consistency: use 1½–2 tablespoons water, see stage 6.

2 Add flavouring, see page 12 for details of various flavourings. If using fruit juice then substitute this for water in stage 1. If using vanilla or other essence then add a few drops only. Do this by dipping a fine skewer into the bottle and allowing the drops to fall into the icing, as in picture above. Tint the icing with culinary colouring, in the same way.

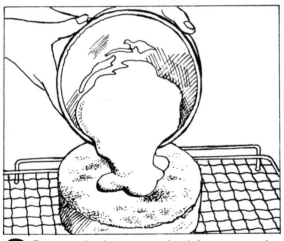

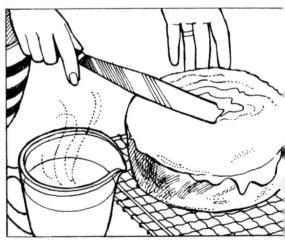

3 Beat well, then pour the icing on to the top of the cake. To keep the icing a good shape on top of the cake use the smaller quantity of water, see stage 1. You will notice that ALL the icing is being poured on to the cake in the picture, this aids in producing an even coating.

4 Spread the fairly stiff icing over the top of the cake with a palette knife, or an icing ruler. Use long sweeping movements. If the icing seems a little too firm to spread easily, dip the knife into hot water, shake or pat dry, but use while warm. Spread the icing from the centre towards the edge of the cake.

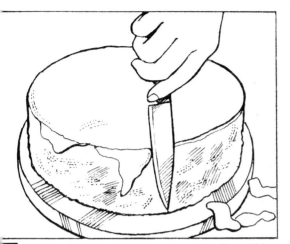

5 Allow the icing to become quite firm. If by chance the icing does drip slightly down the sides of the cake LEAVE IT TO SET. Remove with a very sharp knife as shown in the picture. To coat the top and sides of a cake with glacé icing, follow the same technique as for Royal icing on page 45.

6 If you require an icing that flows over the top and trickles down the sides of the cake, then use the higher proportion of water or other liquid, see stage 1 on the opposite page. This gives a very attractive appearance.

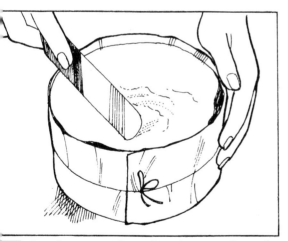

7 Another way of coating the top of a cake with glacé icing is as shown in the picture. Tie a double or treble thickness of greaseproof paper or a band of stiff paper tightly round the cake, secure firmly. This should stand up about $\frac{1}{2}$–1 inch above the cake. Pour the icing on to the cake and allow to become quite set. Remove the paper slowly and carefully, using a warmed knife if necessary.

8 If you wish to make a design on the cake with cherries, angelica, nuts, etc., wait until the glacé icing begins to stiffen. It is a good idea too to 'keep back' about a tablespoon icing in the basin. Dip the cherries, etc., into the icing in the basin, then place them on the half-set coating. If you try and put decorations on a very soft glacé icing they slip out of position and spoil the appearance.

Glacé Icing

The step-by-step instructions on pages 10 and 11 show how simple it is to make and use glacé icing, often called water icing. The basic recipe is repeated on the right, together with the various ways in which it can be flavoured. Below are the approximate quantities you need to give a moderately thick coating for various sized cakes. Obviously the thickness of icing is very much a matter of personal taste; if you like a generous coating then increase the suggested amounts. You will notice that I state it is not essential to sieve the icing sugar for a glacé icing; this only applies if the sugar is fairly smooth. If it has been stored for some time, or in a damp place, and has small hard lumps, then it is wiser to sieve this, or to roll it between two pieces of greaseproof paper.

Quantities needed

Always adjust the amount of water in proportion to that of icing sugar, e.g. 4 oz. icing sugar needs either ¾–1 tablespoon for a soft flowing consistency, or ¾–1 dessertspoon for a firmer consistency, i.e. just half the amount shown in the recipe, right.

To coat top of 6-inch cake, use 4 oz. sugar. To coat top and sides of 6-inch cake (approximate depth 2 inches), use 8–10 oz. sugar. Allow double or rather more than double for top *and* sides — depending upon the depth of the cake. To coat top of 7-inch cake, use 6 oz. sugar. To coat top of 8-inch cake, use 8 oz. sugar. To coat top of 10-inch cake, use 12 oz. sugar.

Plain glacé icing

8 oz. icing sugar   water to mix
                          (see directions)

There are two basic ways of making this icing together with a professional tip, which is given below.

The first and better method is to put the icing sugar and water into a saucepan and to stir over a *very low* heat until well blended. The advantage of using this method is that it produces a better shine to the icing.

The second method is simply to blend the icing sugar and water in a basin until smooth.

The professional method is to blend the icing sugar with sugar syrup, see page 34, in a saucepan. This produces a very high gloss.

For a soft flowing icing, as stage 6, page 11, use about 1½–2 tablespoons water to the 8 oz. icing sugar.

For the firmer icing, shown in stages 3, 4 and 5 on pages 10 and 11, then decrease the amount of water to ¾–1 tablespoon. If you make a mistake in consistency, it is quite easy to remedy this by adding more water or more icing sugar.

Flavourings for glacé icing

The amounts below are for 8 oz. sugar.

Almond, Vanilla, etc: for plain or almond flavoured cakes, etc. Blend a few drops almond or other essence with the icing.

Chocolate: for plain, chocolate or coffee cakes or sponges. Blend 2 oz. melted plain chocolate with icing sugar and little water, or sieve 2 teaspoons cocoa or 1 oz. chocolate powder with icing sugar. About ½ oz. melted butter, or a few drops of oil, give a gloss.

Coffee: for plain, chocolate or coffee cakes or sponges. Mix icing sugar with coffee essence or very strong coffee, or blend 1 teaspoon instant coffee with sugar.

Lemon or Orange: for plain or fruit-flavoured cakes, sponges, etc. Blend sugar with fresh lemon or orange juice.

Liqueur: for plain cakes or sponges. Blend the sugar with half liqueur and half water, tint if wished.

Butter Icing

The step-by-step instructions on pages 14 and 15 show the method of making and using butter icing. This description will be used, although you may like to substitute margarine or white cooking fat (shortening). The basic recipe is given on this page, together with the ways in which it may be flavoured, and an idea of the amount to make to cover various sized cakes. Here are the important rules to remember when making butter icing:

a) always sieve the icing sugar; small lumps will not come out as they are creamed with the butter.

b) never warm the butter, for the icing must be light in texture and if the butter is oiled it spoils the texture, as well as the appearance of the icing.

c) if using an electric mixer, start with a slow speed to prevent the light icing sugar 'flying' in all directions. When the butter and sugar are blended you can increase the speed slightly, but if too high a speed is used the icing will tend to be thrown to the sides of the basin or mixing bowl.

d) if you have made enough icing for coating the cake and for piping, it is a good idea to keep the amount left in the basin for piping covered with a damp paper or cloth so that it does not dry.

Quantities needed

To coat top of 6-inch cake, use 2 oz. butter, 4 oz. icing sugar and flavouring. Allow double for top and filling for 1 layer. Allow at least three times for top, filling and coating sides (depth about 2½ inches). Piping varies very much in the amount it uses, e.g. add 1 oz. butter and 2 oz. sugar for a very narrow band round top of 6-inch cake. To coat top of 7-inch cake, use 3 oz. butter, etc. To coat top of 8-inch cake, use 4 oz. butter, etc. To coat top of 10-inch cake, use 6 oz. butter, etc.

Plain butter icing

2 oz. butter, preferably unsalted
4 oz. icing sugar
flavouring, see below

Cream the butter lightly, then add the sugar and flavouring and beat until soft and light. Keep covered with damp paper or a damp cloth if not ready to use the icing at once; this is particularly important if saving some for piping. The above is the usual proportion for butter icing, but it can be adjusted.

For a firmer consistency that will become crisp: use 6 oz. icing sugar to 2 oz. butter. This may be difficult to spread, and you will need a warm damp knife. For a softer consistency, then use only 3 oz. icing sugar to 2 oz. butter. Do not use less sugar than this, otherwise the mixture will be too greasy.

Flavourings for butter icing

The amounts are for 2 oz. butter and 4 oz. icing sugar.

Almond, Vanilla, etc: suitable for most plain cakes. Blend a few drops almond or other essence with the icing.

Caramel: excellent in plain sponges or in coffee or chocolate cakes, see page 18. Make the caramel as page 70, and use 2 tablespoons, blend with the 2 oz. butter, but add 6 oz. icing sugar.

Chocolate: for plain, coffee or chocolate cakes, etc. Add 1–2 oz. melted and cooled chocolate, or 1 dessertspoon sieved cocoa, or 1 oz. chocolate powder. A few drops vanilla essence can be added if wished.

Coffee: for plain, coffee or chocolate cakes and sponges. Use 1 dessertspoon coffee essence or 1 teaspoon instant coffee.

Lemon or Orange: for plain or fruit-flavoured sponges. Blend the finely grated rind of 1 or 2 lemons or oranges with the icing. Do not use white pith.

Liqueur, etc: a few drops liqueur may be added to the butter icing; or chopped nuts, desiccated coconut, etc., to taste.

Using butter icing

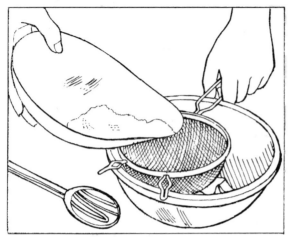

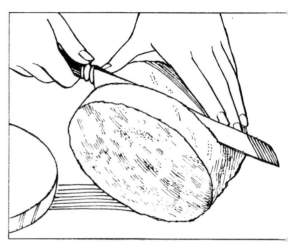

1 Put 2 oz. butter into the basin or mixing bowl, add 4 oz. sieved icing sugar and any flavouring, see page 13, and beat with a wooden spoon until soft and light. In cold weather it is a good idea to cream the butter and flavouring, then add the sugar gradually. See page 13 for directions on using a mixer.

2 If filling one cake: cut into layers across the cake. Use a cake knife for this so you have even slices. Spread with the butter icing and sandwich together. Fit the layers carefully to give a perfect shape to the cake. Sponge sandwiches are just sandwiched together. Make sure there is no icing around the edges.

3 To coat the top of a cake with butter icing, put the whole amount on the top of the cake, then spread out with long sweeping movements with a palette knife or icing ruler. Remember you never have quite the smooth shine on top of the cake that you would have with glacé icing; this is why butter icing is often used for the filling, and glacé icing as the top coating.

4 If coating the sides of a cake with butter icing, do this BEFORE covering the top, unless you have an icing table, when you can spread from the top down the sides. Spread the icing roughly over all the sides, then neaten with a palette knife or icing ruler, see stage 6. After this, cover the top as stage 3.

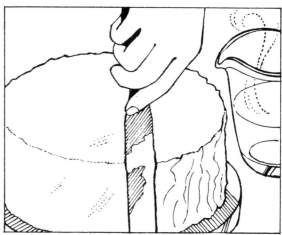

5 The picture above shows the way to coat the top and sides of a cake with butter icing when you have a turn-table, or are using an upturned basin. Put ALL the butter icing for coating on the top of the cake then sweep this from the centre of the top down the sides. Coat the cake completely, then neaten as stage 6.

6 The picture above shows the way to hold the palette knife to give a smooth coating to the sides, i.e. holding the knife upright against the cake and using a gentle 'dragging' movement.

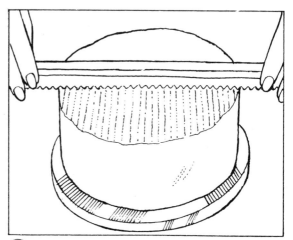

7 A cake coated with butter icing is fairly 'sticky' that is why it is often coated with nuts, etc., at the sides, and perhaps on top too. The picture on page 6 shows how to coat the sides of a cake with chopped nuts. Follow this for coating the sides, then spread the top with butter icing and sprinkle on the nuts, etc. Press gently, as shown in the picture, with a palette knife.

8 The top can, however, be given a simple design by marking with the prongs of a fork or the serrated edge of an icing ruler, as shown in the picture above. If you use a fairly generous amount of sugar as suggested on page 13, the top icing becomes almost crisp. For piping instructions see page 48.

Family Cakes

The cake recipes you will find in the next few pages are quick and economical, and therefore ideal for family tea-time. The icing or topping makes them look particularly interesting.

Some of the cakes are prepared within minutes, for they are based on the one-stage mixing method, made possible by using one of the modern soft margarines or cooking fats (shortenings). Instead of creaming the fat and sugar for some minutes, then adding the flour, etc. gradually, ALL the ingredients are put into the mixing bowl together. If using an electric mixer they need beating for about 1 minute only, until blended and soft. This will take approximately 3 minutes by hand. Page 18 gives hints on obtaining the best results from this quick-mix method.

Because many family cakes use a small amount of fat they do not keep moist for a long period. Each cake recipe therefore gives the time for storage, so that you may enjoy it at its best.

Where recipes state 'flour' they mean self-raising flour. Where they state 'sugar' it can be castor or granulated sugar.

Victoria sandwich

6 oz. table margarine
6 oz. castor sugar
3 eggs (large if possible)*

6 oz. flour (with plain flour use 1½ level teaspoons baking powder)

* see comments about size of eggs, etc., in the method

Cream the margarine and sugar until soft and light. If preferred use butter or a white fat (shortening). Beat the eggs in a bowl, and add a little egg to the creamed mixture. Continue to beat in the eggs slowly, so the margarine mixture does not curdle. If it shows signs of this, i.e separating, add a little sieved flour at once. Fold in the sieved flour, or flour and baking powder very gently with a metal spoon. The mixture should be the consistency of a thick cream. I the eggs are a little small then add enough wate to give this consistency. Divide the mixture evenly between two 7–8-inch greased and floured sandwich tins, and bake just above the centre of a moderate oven for about 25 minutes

A Victoria sandwich, or butter sponge, as it is often called, seems to reflect inconsistencies o ovens almost more than any other cake. The temperature should be between 350–375°F. Gas Mark 4–5, but do follow the instructions for oven setting and position given by the cooker manufacturer. Test to see if cooked by pressing gently but firmly in the centre of the cake; if no impression is left by your finger the cake is ready to come out of the oven. Turn ou of the tins carefully on to a wire cooling tray If not quite level on top it does mean that you probably used too little moisture, and the cake rose slightly to a 'peak'. If this is the case, then use the base of the sandwich as the top, so giving a flat base for icing, etc.

If preferred, bake this mixture in one 7–8-inch cake tin for approximately 50 minutes in the centre of a very moderate oven, 325–350°F. Gas Mark 3–4. It is a good idea to do this if you wish to ice only the top of the cake, also you can split one sponge cake into as many layer as wished.

A Victoria sandwich is an ideal basis for man iced cakes, see pages 17–19.

Quantities needed

For a 6–7-inch sandwich or cake, use 4 oz. margarine, etc., this is often called a 2-egg mixture. Bake sandwich cakes for about 20 minutes, and a deeper cake for about 40 minutes; temperatures and oven positions as recipe on previous page.

For an 8–9-inch sandwich or cake, use 8 oz. margarine, etc., this is often called a 4-egg mixture. Bake sandwich cakes for about 30 minutes, and a deeper cake for about 1 hour (you may need to reduce the heat slightly after 30 minutes). The temperatures and oven positions should be as recipe on previous page.

Economical Victoria sandwich

oz. table margarine	6 oz. flour (with plain flour
oz. castor sugar	use 1½ level teaspoons
eggs (large if possible)	baking powder)
	water to mix

Use the method of mixing as the true Victoria sandwich on the previous page, but add enough water to give the correct consistency. Bake as the Victoria sandwich, but you will find you can have a *very slightly* higher oven setting and a *slightly shorter* cooking time.

The true Victoria sandwich should keep well for about 1 week, for icing and fillings help to keep it moist. This assumes you have a good cake tin that excludes the air, or you wrap a plain cake in plenty of foil or polythene (icings may stick to these). The economical cake, immediately above, should be eaten within a few days. A sponge, as page 16, freezes well with or without the icing and fillings, but does tend to become a little firmer in texture.

Flavourings to use

The recipes that follow give a variety of flavourings, and show how the basic recipe must be adapted. If you just wish to use spices though, there is no need to change the proportions of flour, etc. Use spices (i.e. cinnamon, nutmeg) sparingly to keep a delicate flavour.

Coconut layer cake

ingredients as the true	filling and topping
Victoria sandwich, page	8 oz. butter or margarine
16, or the economical	12 oz. sieved icing sugar
version, page 17, or the	4 oz. desiccated coconut
coconut cake, page 20.	about 1 oz. glacé cherries

Make the sponge sandwich or cake as recipe, allow to cool before decorating. Make the butter icing as page 13. The proportions are slightly different in this recipe, as these suit the cake. Spoon one-third of the mixture into a second basin, add 2 oz. coconut. Put 3 or 4 cherries on one side, chop the rest and add to the coconut mixture. Sandwich the cakes together with this; split a deep cake into two layers then sandwich together. Coat the sides of the cake with just over half the butter icing, and roll in the coconut as page 6. Spread the remainder of the butter icing on top, then sprinkle with the last of the coconut. Decorate with the halved cherries. The coconut filling and coating help this cake to keep moist for up to 10 days if well covered, or stored in an air-tight tin.

Coffee layer sponge

	filling
5 oz. butter or table	2 oz. butter or margarine
margarine	4 oz. sieved icing sugar
5 oz. castor sugar	2 teaspoons sweetened
3 small eggs	coffee essence
1 tablespoon sweetened	
coffee essence	icing
6 oz. flour (with plain flour	6 oz. sieved icing sugar
use 1½ level teaspoons	1–2 teaspoons sweetened
baking powder)	coffee essence
	little water

Cream the butter or margarine and sugar until soft and light. Gradually beat in the eggs and coffee essence as Victoria sandwich, page 16, then fold in the sieved flour. Bake in two 7–8-inch greased and floured sandwich tins, or one cake tin as the Victoria sandwich. Allow to cool before decorating. Cream the butter or margarine, icing sugar and coffee essence together. Sandwich the cakes with the butter icing, or split one deep cake into two layers and sandwich together. Make the glacé icing as pages 10–12, adding the coffee essence to personal taste and about 1 tablespoon water. Spread neatly on top of the sponge, leave to set. Eat within 1 week.

Chocolate layer sponge

6 oz. butter or table
    margarine
6 oz. castor sugar
3 large eggs
5½ oz. flour (with plain flour
    use 1½ level teaspoons
    baking powder)
1 tablespoon cocoa

filling
¼ pint thick cream
2 oz. plain chocolate

icing
2 oz. plain chocolate
about ¼ oz. butter

Cream the butter or margarine and sugar until soft and light. Gradually add the eggs as the Victoria sandwich page 16. Sieve the flour and cocoa. If you wish a stronger chocolate flavour use 5 oz. flour and 1 oz. cocoa. Fold the flour and cocoa into the butter or margarine mixture, adding a very little water if the mixture is too stiff. Divide between two 7–8-inch sandwich tins, or one deep cake tin, and bake as the Victoria sandwich. Allow to cool before decorating. Whip the cream until it just holds its shape. Chop or grate the chocolate for filling, and add to the cream. Sandwich the two cakes with this, or split one cake, then sandwich together. To ice, melt the chocolate, as page 43, stage 1, with the butter (glycerine or olive oil can be used instead). Cool a little, then spread over the top of the cake and allow to harden. As cream is very perishable, eat when fresh.

If preferred, sandwich the cakes with plain or chocolate-flavoured butter icing, as page 13. Top with chocolate glacé icing, page 12, or chocolate butter icing, page 13, and chopped nuts. Keeps well then for 10 days. A plain Victoria sandwich is also excellent filled with jam and cream, and topped with melted chocolate.

Mocha layer sponge

ingredients as chocolate
    layer cake, recipe above

filling and icing
as coffee layer sponge,
    page 17

Make the chocolate cake as above, then sandwich with the coffee butter icing and top with the coffee glacé icing. This combination of chocolate and coffee is very good. If preferred, make the coffee cake as page 17, and sandwich together with chocolate butter icing as page 13, and top either with more chocolate butter icing, chocolate-flavoured glacé icing, page 12, or melted chocolate.

Orange layer sponge

5 oz. butter or table
    margarine
6 oz. castor sugar
2 teaspoons finely grated
    orange rind
3 medium eggs
6 oz. flour (with plain flour
    use 1½ level teaspoons
    baking powder)
1 tablespoon orange juice

filling
3 oz. butter
6 oz. sieved icing sugar
1 teaspoon finely grated
    orange rind

icing
6 oz. sieved icing sugar
1 tablespoon orange juice
few drops yellow colouring

Cream the butter or margarine, sugar and orange rind together until soft and light. Gradually add the eggs (see Victoria sandwich page 16) then fold in the sieved flour and the orange juice. Divide the mixture between two prepared 7–8-inch sandwich tins, or one cake tin, and bake as Victoria sandwich. This could be served plain, or sandwich the cakes together with the butter icing, made by creaming the butter sugar and orange rind until soft. Split one cake to make two layers and sandwich together. Blend the icing sugar, orange juice and a few drops colouring to give a pleasant pale orange colour. Spread over the top of the cake and allow to set. This keeps for about 1 week.

Orange chocolate sponge

Use the orange sponge above, then sandwich together with chocolate butter icing, page 13. Top either with melted chocolate or with chocolate glacé icing, page 12.

Orange almond sponge

Use the orange sponge sandwich or cake, as recipe above, and bake as Victoria sandwich on page 16. Make up the orange butter icing with 9 oz. butter, 1 lb. 2 oz. sieved icing sugar and teaspoons *finely grated* orange rind. Sandwich the cakes together with just under one-third of the butter icing. Blanch and chop 3 oz. almonds. Coat the sides with half the butter icing left, roll in some of the nuts, as page 6. Top the cake with butter icing and nuts, then decorate with little piping in the centre of the cake, if wished. The moist filling and coating helps to keep the cake soft for about 10 days.

Chocolate layer cake – Chocolate Victoria sandwich, page 17, bake 4 layers. Make each layer with 4 oz. butter or margarine, etc., sandwich with three layers chocolate butter icing and coat with the same icing.

Almond cake

4 oz. margarine or butter
4 oz. castor sugar
4 oz. flour (with plain flour use 1 level teaspoon baking powder)
2 oz. ground almonds
few drops almond essence
2 large eggs
2 teaspoons milk

Cream the margarine or butter and sugar until soft and light. Sieve the flour or flour and baking powder, mix with the ground almonds. Add the almond essence and the beaten eggs gradually to the creamed mixture, then fold in the flour and ground almonds and the milk. Put into a well greased and floured 7-inch cake tin and bake in the centre of a slow to very moderate oven, 300–325°F., Gas Mark 2–3, for approximately 1¼ hours. This is a cake that should keep well for up to 2 weeks.

Decorations for almond cake

This is a basic cake you can decorate in a variety of ways:

a) with sugar: sprinkle castor sugar on the cake before baking.

b) with almonds: blanch about 1 oz. almonds, see below, split lengthways (so they are not too heavy), then arrange on top of the cake before baking. If possible brush with a little egg white (that left in the shell) to give a glaze.

c) with almond glacé icing: blend 6 oz. icing sugar with just under 1 tablespoon warm water and a few drops almond essence, see pages 10–12. Coat top of cake, decorate with whole blanched almonds, see below.

d) with almond butter icing: cream 3 oz. butter and 5 oz. sieved icing sugar with a few drops of almond essence. Spread this over the top of the cake, and sprinkle top with about 2 oz. chopped blanched almonds.

To blanch almonds

Put the almonds into a strong basin or other container. Cover them with boiling water. Leave for a minute, then lift out with a spoon. Cool, remove the skins and dry before using.

Coconut cake

4 oz. margarine or butter or cooking fat (shortening)
6 oz. castor sugar*
2 large eggs
6 oz. flour (with plain flour use 1½ level teaspoons baking powder)
2 oz. desiccated coconut
4 tablespoons milk

* this high percentage of sugar gives a very light cake; reduce to 4 oz. if wished

Cream the margarine or butter, or fat, with 4 oz. sugar until soft and light. Separate the eggs, and beat the yolks gradually into the fat mixture. Sieve the flour, or flour and baking powder, and mix with the coconut. Stir the flour mixture and milk alternately into the fat and egg yolks. Whisk the egg whites stiffly, then gradually whisk in rest of sugar. Fold into the cake, then spoon this mixture carefully into a 7-inch cake tin, lined with greased greaseproof paper. Bake in the centre of a very moderate oven, 325–350°F., Gas Mark 3–4, for approximately 55 minutes. Reduce heat after about 30 minutes if cake is getting too brown. Turn out carefully. The cake is at its best for only about 48 hours.

Decorations for coconut cake

There are a variety of ways in which this cake may be decorated; watch any adjustments of the basic recipe as suggested below.

a) with sugar: sprinkle castor sugar on the cake before baking.

b) with sugar and coconut: sprinkle a thin layer of desiccated coconut then a little sugar on the cake before baking. Coconut browns quickly, so lower the heat rather early and allow a little longer cooking.

c) coconut layer cake: see page 17.

d) coconut ice cake: blend 2 oz. desiccated coconut with enough sweetened condensed milk to give a sticky consistency (about 2 tablespoons). Allow the cake to cool slightly, spread with the mixture and brown under a grill, set to a low heat.

e) coconut streusel topping: do not separate eggs; use 3 tablespoons milk only in cake, to give firmer consistency. Blend 2 oz. margarine, 3 oz. sugar, 2 oz. flour, 2 oz. desiccated coconut. Press on the cake and bake as above, allowing 1¼ hours.

Orange cake

1½ oz. margarine or cooking
   fat (shortening)
3 oz. sugar
3 tablespoons orange juice
6 oz. flour (with plain flour
   use 1½ level teaspoons
   baking powder)

3 eggs

filling
3 oz. sieved icing sugar
2 tablespoons orange
   marmalade

Put the margarine or fat, sugar and orange juice into a saucepan. Heat gently until the margarine or fat has melted. Sieve the flour, or flour and baking powder, into a bowl, add the orange mixture and beat well. Gradually stir in the beaten eggs. Line the bottom of two 7-inch sandwich tins with rounds of well greased and floured greaseproof paper, and grease and flour the sides. Put in the mixture and bake just above the centre of a moderate oven, 350–375°F., Gas Mark 4–5, for about 20 minutes until firm to the touch. Turn out and allow to cool. Blend the icing sugar and marmalade together, if the marmalade has large pieces of peel, chop these finely. Sandwich the cakes with the marmalade filling. This cake should be eaten within 2 days.

Variations on orange cake

To give a stronger orange flavour, add about 2 teaspoons grated orange rind to the basic mixture above.

Iced orange cake: blend 6 oz. icing sugar and about 1 tablespoon orange juice and spread over the cake. Decorate with several crystallised orange slices.

Lemon or tangerine juice, etc., could be used in place of orange juice.

Using an electric mixer for cakes

A mixer will help in making cakes, as well as in the preparation of icings. It is important though that flour is not over-beaten in a cake. Use the mixer for creaming fat, sugar and eggs, also for whisking egg whites, but in most cakes it is better to incorporate the flour by hand. Over-beating of flour in a sponge spoils the light texture, and helps to make the cake crack in the case of fruit cakes.

Ginger sponge parkin

6 oz. flour (with plain flour
   use 1½ level teaspoons
   baking powder)
1 teaspoon powdered
   ginger
2 oz. margarine
2 oz. sugar
2 tablespoons golden syrup
5 tablespoons milk
½ level teaspoon
   bicarbonate of soda

filling
2 oz. butter or margarine
3 oz. sieved icing sugar
1 oz. preserved ginger

icing
6 oz. icing sugar
1 tablespoon water*
little preserved ginger

* or just a little syrup from the preserved ginger, plus water to give 1 tablespoon

Sieve together the flour, or flour and baking powder, with the ginger. Rub in the margarine and add the sugar. Warm the syrup in a saucepan, add to the flour, etc., then warm the milk in the same saucepan. Stir the bicarbonate of soda into this until dissolved. Add to the flour mixture and beat well. Line a 7-inch cake tin with well greased and floured greaseproof paper. Put in the mixture. Bake in the centre of a very moderate oven, 325–350°F., Gas Mark 3–4, for about 50 minutes. Reduce the heat slightly after 35 minutes if necessary. Turn out carefully and cool, then split through the centre and sandwich together with the filling mixture. To make this, cream the butter or margarine and icing sugar, then add the chopped ginger. Top the cake with a layer of glacé icing, made by blending the icing sugar and water, or ginger syrup and water. When nearly set, put the pieces of sliced preserved ginger on the cake for decoration. This cake, although economical, keeps for about 1 week.

Peanut butter sponge parkin

Use peanut butter in cake and filling, instead of fat in above recipe.

Honey sponge parkin

Follow the recipe for ginger sponge parkin but omit the ginger. Add the finely grated rind of 1 lemon instead. Use 2 tablespoons clear honey in place of golden syrup, and 2 tablespoons cold lemon juice and 3 of warm milk in place of 5 tablespoons milk. Flavour filling and icing with lemon, omit the ginger.

Austrian streusel cake

8 oz. plain flour	**topping**
pinch salt	3 oz. butter or margarine
grated rind 1 lemon	4 oz. sugar
2 oz. sugar	4 oz. flour
½ oz. fresh yeast or ¼ oz.	½–1 teaspoon cinnamon
dried yeast	
5 tablespoons milk	
4 oz. butter or margarine	

Sieve the flour and salt into a warm bowl, add grated lemon rind and all the sugar but 1 tea-spoonful. Keep in a warm place. Cream the tea-spoon of sugar with the fresh yeast, add *tepid* milk.

If using dried yeast, warm the milk, add the sugar, sprinkle the yeast on top. Make a 'well' in the centre of the bowl of flour, pour in the yeast liquid and sprinkle a little flour over this. Cover the bowl with a cloth, leave in a warm place for 15–20 minutes if using fresh yeast, or a little longer with dried yeast, until the top of the mix-ture is covered with bubbles. While this is happening, melt the butter or margarine and allow it to cool to blood heat. Pour into the bowl and mix all the ingredients together with a palette knife. Turn on to a floured board, knead with the tips of your fingers until smooth. To tell if sufficiently kneaded, press with a floured finger and the mark should come out. Return the mixture to the bowl and leave in a warm place, covered with a cloth, for about 45 minutes, to allow the dough to 'prove', i.e. rise to about twice its original size. Knead again, then put into a greased and floured 8-inch square or 9-inch round tin, press out so the dough fits the tin neatly. Put all the ingredients for the topping into a bowl, beat together, then spread over the top of the cake. Cover the tin with a cloth and leave to 'prove' for about 25 minutes, bake in the centre of a moderate to moderately hot oven, 375–400°F., Gas Mark 5–6, for 20 minutes, then lower the heat to very moderate for a further 15–20 minutes, until firm. This cake must be eaten when fresh.

Fruit streusel cake

Add 2 oz. sultanas, 1 oz. chopped peel and 1 oz. chopped glacé cherries to the flour, etc., in the recipe above. Bake as basic recipe, but allow slightly longer to 'prove'.

Lemon streusel cake

Use the grated rind and juice of 1 lemon in the basic recipe. Measure lemon juice, then add milk to make up to 5 tablespoons. Omit the cinnamon from the topping. When the cake is cooked, and cool, pour a soft flowing glacé icing over the top. Make this with 6 oz. of icing sugar and 1½ tablespoons lemon juice – it must be a very thin coating. Allow to set, and eat when fresh.

Assorted fancy cakes
(see picture opposite)

Make Victoria sandwich as page 16, with 4 eggs etc. Bake as page 16, but in an oblong tin about 11 by 8 inches, lined with greased greaseproof paper, to stand above the sides and support the cake as it rises. Cool, and cut into the shapes below. Any trimmings may be used in trifles, or crisped and used instead of crisp breadcrumbs in Crumb gâteau, page 71. All the icings mentioned are in this book.

Cauliflower cakes: cut out rounds, coat with sieved apricot jam and bands of green tinted marzipan. Pipe tiny rosettes of whipped cream or vanilla butter icing, on top.

Orange coffee fingers: cut fingers, brush with marmalade or orange curd. Coat sides with chopped walnuts. Pipe coffee butter icing or whipped cream, flavoured with instant coffee powder, on top. Decorate with well drained canned mandarin oranges.

Chocolate whirligigs: cut rounds, brush the sides with apricot jam or with vanilla butter icing, roll in chocolate vermicelli. Spread the tops of each cake with vanilla butter icing, pipe a border, decorate with triangles of chocolate (see page 32).

Raspberry diamonds: coat diamond shapes with raspberry flavoured glacé icing and coat the sides with chopped nuts. When the icing is firm pipe as picture.

Pineapple gâteaux: prepare shape as Chocolate whirligigs above, to the size of rings of glacé or well drained pineapple. To coat, turn cake and pineapple gently in a shallow dish of melted chocolate. Allow to set and decorate with glacé cherries.

Walnut triangles: coat triangles with vanilla butter icing, coat the sides with chopped walnuts and decorate with curls, caraque of chocolate, as page 43.

Assorted fancy cakes

Easy Small Cakes

All the small cakes in this chapter are very easy and are based mainly on the creamed mixture, similar to a Victoria sponge sandwich on page 16. Remember that small cakes dry easily, so they should be baked fairly quickly to ensure they are as moist as possible when they come from the oven.

Glacé and butter icings, detailed from page 10 to page 15, are ideal toppings for small cakes; decorations such as glacé cherries, angelica, small silver balls, etc., can make them look most interesting.

If you wish to make cup cakes, then buy paper cases in which to bake the cakes. To keep these a good shape support the paper cases (as suggested in the recipe) in patty tins.

Cup cakes

2 oz. butter or margarine
2 oz. castor sugar
1 large egg
2 oz. flour (with plain flour use ½ teaspoon baking powder)

icing
6 oz. icing sugar
1 tablespoon water
flavouring, see page 12 for suggestions

Cream the butter or margarine and sugar until soft and light. Gradually beat in the egg, then add the sieved flour, or flour and baking powder. The mixture must be a soft consistency, otherwise the cakes will not rise level on top. If in doubt add a few drops milk, water or fruit juice. Put about 12 paper cake cases into plain round patty tins or bun tins; this supports the paper cases and prevents the cakes becoming a bad shape. Half fill each case with the mixture, and bake towards the top of a moderately hot oven, 400°F., Gas Mark 5–6, for 10–12 minutes, until firm. Do not bake quite as quickly as plain buns (see next column) for you do not wish the cakes to rise into a peak. Allow the cakes to cool, then spoon a good layer of icing on top of each one. To make this, just mix the ingredients together. Allow 1–2 hours for the icing to dry, since it will be fairly thick. If preferred use a flowing fondant which hardens more quickly, see page 35. Eat most cup cakes within 2 days.

Note. The one-stage method of mixing, as described on the next page, is ideal for the simple cup cakes. Do not add extra baking powder though, as these cakes should be flat.

Banana cup cakes

Cream the butter or margarine and sugar as above, add 1 mashed ripe banana, 1 tablespoon lemon juice. Beat in 1 small egg and 3 oz. sieved flour, or flour and ¾ teaspoon baking powder. Bake as above, filling about 15 small cases, then top with lemon-flavoured glacé icing, see page 12. Eat same day.

Chocolate cup cakes

Remove 2 teaspoons flour from basic recipe, add 2 teaspoons cocoa, sieve with the flour.

Madeleines

Butterfly cakes

Use the same recipe as for cup cakes, using only a small egg or 3 oz. flour to the same proportions of margarine and sugar. This makes sure the cakes will rise to a peak. Bake the cakes towards the top of a hot oven, 425–450°F., Gas Mark 6–7, for just 9–10 minutes. Cut a slice from the top of each cake, divide this into two portions. These are the 'wings'. Spread the top of the cakes with whipped cream (you need about $\frac{1}{4}$ pint), or butter icing made with 2 oz. butter, 4 oz. sieved icing sugar and a few drops vanilla essence. Press the 'wings' gently into position and dust the tops of the cakes with sieved icing sugar. Eat within 2 days.

Cherry buns

As cup cakes; use 3 oz. flour, add 2 oz. chopped glacé cherries. Bake in the paper cases as for cup cakes. When cooked top with glacé icing, made with only 4 oz. icing sugar and $\frac{3}{4}$ tablespoon water, and with halved glacé cherries. Alternatively, omit glacé icing and place a teaspoonful of jam on top of each, then pipe butter icing round the edge (see picture on jacket). Eat within 2 to 3 days.

One stage cake mixtures

There is no need to select special recipes for one stage mixtures. Any of the recipes from page 16 onwards can be used. Use one of the quick creaming margarines (often called 'soft' or 'luxury') or the soft white fats (shortenings). Put all the ingredients in the bowl of an electric mixer, or an ordinary large bowl or basin. Switch on to low speed, blend for about 1 minute; or beat well with a wooden spoon for 2–3 minutes, or until soft. As less air is beaten into the mixture it is wise to add an extra $\frac{1}{2}$–1 teaspoon baking powder to each 4–6 oz. flour. This tends to make the cakes dry out and become stale a little more quickly, so use while fresh.

Madeleines

Use the recipe for cup cakes, i.e. a soft mixture, so the cakes rise with a level top in the tins. Dariole tins are fairly deep so 2 oz. butter, etc., will make about 8–9 cakes.

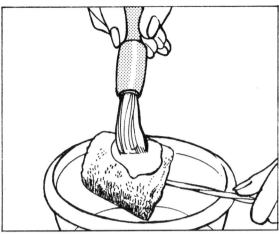

1 Bake the mixture in greased dariole (castle pudding) tins until firm. Turn out and allow to cool. Brush with sieved warm jam or warm jelly. The easiest way to do this is to insert a fine skewer into each cake and turn this round as you coat with a pastry brush, dipped in the jam.

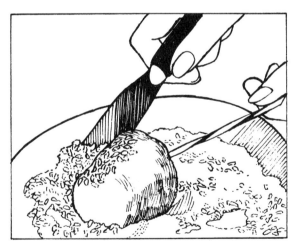

2 Either put the coconut on a plate or into a paper bag. If using a plate, turn the cakes on the skewer in this, or coat evenly with the help of two knives. If using a bag put the cakes in with the base uppermost as this should NOT be coated. When the cakes are evenly coated, top with halved glacé cherries and leaves of angelica. Brush the under-side of these with a little jam to make sure they 'stick' to the cakes. Will keep about 10 days.

Light as a Feather

The cakes in this chapter are particularly light and delicate in texture. They include the classic sponge (a favourite in most countries) and the American Angel cake, with interesting variations on this. Some equally light and well known Continental gâteaux, and a variety of original recipes start on page 66.

Each cake has the filling and icing that is traditional, or which, in my opinion, blends best. If you wish to change the icing, then select one that is not too heavy for the cake.

Sponge cake

2 large eggs	2 oz. flour, either self-
3 oz. castor sugar	raising or plain

Put the eggs and sugar into a mixing bowl, and whisk sharply until sufficiently thick to see the mark of the whisk. Sieve the flour at least once, and fold into the eggs and sugar with a metal spoon, or palette knife, until evenly blended. The method of making this cake incorporates so much air that a raising agent is not really essential, but until you *are sure* you have the right technique it is a good idea to sieve ½ teaspoon baking powder with plain flour. The mixture should be very soft, so fold in 1 dessertspoon hot water after the flour if you find it rather thick, this of course depends upon the size of the eggs.

Grease and flour two 6–7-inch sandwich tins, or one deeper cake tin, or line with greased greaseproof paper. Bake the sandwich cakes towards the top of a moderately hot oven, 400°F., Gas Mark 5–6, or you may prefer to get the oven a little hotter, then turn it down to moderate and bake the cake, this seems to give a sponge a more 'fluffy' texture. Allow about 12–14 minutes cooking time. With one cake though, bake in the centre of a very moderate to moderate oven, 350°F., Gas Mark 3–4, for about 25–30 minutes. This is a cake that browns very readily and will dry if overcooked, so test early by pressing on top very gently, but firmly, to see if ready. The first time you bake this, watch the oven carefully, as these vary so much and can over-brown this cake quicker than anticipated. Turn out on to sugared paper or a wire cooling tray, and cool away from a draught. As this is a delicate textured cake, all fillings and decorations need to be soft. Cakes based on this recipe must be eaten when fresh.

Quantities needed

For a 7–8-inch sandwich or cake, use 3 eggs, etc., and bake for a few minutes longer than the times given above. For a 9–10-inch cake or sandwich, use 4 eggs, etc. Bake sandwiches for 18–20 minutes, and one cake for about 40 minutes. Choose a slightly lower temperature for these larger cakes, and reduce the heat after about 20 minutes if necessary.

Crystal cake – A light sponge coated with butter icing (see pages 1
Make caramel icing as page 70, but pour this on to a slab to form s⁺
Mark out pieces when nearly set, and when firm put on to the cake.

Vanilla sponge

ingredients as sponge recipe, page 26

filling
2 tablespoons jam
¼ pint thick cream
few drops vanilla essence
½–1 oz. castor sugar

icing and decoration
4 oz. icing sugar
few drops vanilla essence
¾ tablespoon water

crystallised rose petals
little angelica

Make the sponge as page 26, allow to cool. Spread one half with jam. Whip the cream until it just holds a shape, fold in vanilla and sugar and whip sharply once or twice. Spread over the jam, but do not put the second cake on top, as it is easier to spread the icing before sandwiching on to the soft cream. Make the glacé icing with the vanilla and water. Spread over the second cake, then lift on to the first sponge very carefully. Do this before the icing begins to set, otherwise it will crack. Allow to become nearly stiff, then place rose petals and leaves of angelica in position. The recipe for crystallising rose petals, etc., is on page 76.

To make 'leaves' of angelica, cut diamond shapes. If the angelica is very hard and 'sugary' then rinse in warm water and dry.

Lemon sponge

Make the sponge cake, page 26, fill with lemon-flavoured butter icing, page 13, using 2 oz. butter, etc., but make a little softer than usual with a small amount of lemon juice. Spread the top of the cake with lemon glacé icing, see page 12, using 4 oz. icing sugar, etc. Orange juice, etc., can be used instead.

To give a more pronounced orange or lemon flavour, add a little finely grated fruit rind to the eggs and sugar in the sponge mixture, and fold in hot fruit juice instead of water, see page 26.

Chocolate cream sponge

Follow recipe for sponge, page 26, substitute 2–3 teaspoons *sieved* cocoa for same amount of flour. Fill with whipped cream or butter icing made with 2 oz. butter, etc., page 13. Top with 3–4 oz. melted chocolate, page 43.

Swiss roll

2 large eggs
3 oz. castor sugar
2 oz. flour, either self-raising or plain
½–1 tablespoon water

coating
little castor sugar

filling
3–4 tablespoons jam

Make the sponge by whisking the eggs and sugar together as page 26. The consistency of the mixture for a Swiss roll should be a little softer than a sandwich or cake, so that it flows easily. Add the hot water to the mixture, after the flour. Pour into a small sized Swiss roll tin, about 8 inches by 11–12 inches, lined with well greased greaseproof paper. Bake for approximately 7–9 minutes towards the top of a hot oven, 425–450°F., Gas Mark 6–7. Test early to see if cooked, by pressing gently but firmly in the centre of the sponge. If no impression is left, then the cake is cooked. Over-cooking makes it very difficult to roll the sponge. While the sponge is cooking, shake a layer of castor sugar on a sheet of greaseproof paper and warm the jam, do not overheat this. Turn the sponge on to the sugared paper, cut away the edges if they are slightly crisp. Spread with the warm jam, then make a shallow cut across the sponge, about ½ inch from the end nearest to you. Fold this over firmly, then roll the sponge by lifting the sugared paper and using this to form the sponge into a neat roll. Cool away from a draught. Keeps 2 days. (See below.)

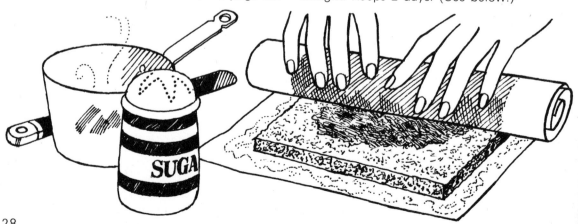

Cream filled Swiss roll

ingredients as Swiss roll, page 28

coating
little castor sugar

filling
2-3 tablespoons jam (optional)
¼ pint thick cream

Make the Swiss roll as page 28. Turn on to the sugared paper, then roll firmly with the paper rolled into the sponge. This makes sure it will not crack when it is unrolled again to fill. If you find it easier, lay a second sheet of greaseproof paper over the plain sponge and roll with this inside. Allow to cool, then unroll. Spread with the cold jam (do not use too much) and the firmly whipped cream, then re-roll again. If preferred, butter icing made with 2 oz. butter, etc., as page 13, may be used instead of cream.

Chocolate cream roll

ingredients as Swiss roll, page 28, but substitute 2-3 teaspoons *sieved* cocoa for the same amount of flour. It makes a particularly delicious cake if about 2 oz. chopped chocolate and a few drops of Tia Maria, or rum, are added to the ¼ pint whipped cream before filling the roll; omit jam if wished, see recipe above.

Coffee walnut roll

ingredients as Swiss roll, page 28, but use about ½ tablespoon coffee essence warmed with ½ tablespoon water, instead of all water. If preferred, use 1 tablespoon very strong coffee. Roll the sponge round greaseproof paper as the first recipe above. Make coffee butter icing with 4 oz. butter, 8 oz. sieved icing sugar and ½-1 tablespoon coffee essence, or 1–2 teaspoons instant coffee blended with a little water. The butter icing must not be too stiff as it would break the delicate cake. Add 1–2 oz. chopped walnuts to half the icing. Unroll the sponge, spread with the walnut filling. Roll firmly. Coat the outside of the roll with the rest of the butter icing, and sprinkle with another 2 oz. chopped walnuts. Press these firmly against the icing with a palette knife.

Marzipan roll

ingredients as Swiss roll, page 28

coating
little castor sugar

filling
3 oz. ground almonds
few drops almond essence
4 oz. sieved icing sugar
1 small egg
1-2 oz. glacé cherries

Make the Swiss roll as page 28. Turn on to the sugared paper and spread with the very soft marzipan filling and roll firmly. To make the marzipan filling, put the ground almonds into a basin with the almond essence and sugar. Add enough of the beaten egg to give a mixture like a thick cream, add the chopped glacé cherries. The sponge may be spread with a little warm apricot jam before the marzipan. Details of various other kinds of marzipan are on page 39.

Bûche de Noël

ingredients as Swiss roll, page 28

coating
little castor sugar

filling and icing
4 oz. butter or margarine
8 oz. sieved icing sugar
1 oz. chocolate powder
½ tablespoon strong coffee
little extra icing sugar

Make the Swiss roll as page 28. Turn on to the sugared paper and roll round the greaseproof paper. Allow to cool. Make up the butter icing with both chocolate and coffee to flavour. Unroll the sponge, spread with just about half the mixture and roll again. Spread the rest of the filling thickly over the roll, and mark 'ridges' down the roll, to look like the markings on a tree trunk. Do this with a fine skewer or prongs of a fork. Dust with sieved icing sugar along the top to look like snow. This is the simplest way to make this cake, traditional in France as a Christmas cake. It can be varied in many ways. To make a more interesting shape, put a small 'branch' against the side of the cake, this can be made with marzipan. Coat the main roll and the small piece with the icing, as above, then decorate with tiny holly leaves and a robin.

Chestnut filling: this is one of the most popular fillings for this roll. Add about 3 oz. fresh or canned sieved chestnut purée to the filling of chocolate, etc., above.

Angel cake

3 oz. self-raising or plain
flour
7 oz. castor sugar
whites 6 large eggs

pinch of cream of tartar
few drops vanilla essence
few drops almond essence

Sieve the flour 2 or 3 times, and put in a warm place, for this helps to lighten it. When ready to make the cake, sieve the flour with half the sugar. Whisk the whites of eggs until they JUST stand in peaks. Be careful not to over-beat if using an electric mixer. Whisk in the rest of the sugar, cream of tartar and essences. Fold the flour and sugar mixture very carefully into the egg whites. The mixture should be very light and fluffy in the bowl; if it seems rather dry fold in about ½ tablespoon warm water after the flour. This is baked in an Angel cake tin, which is a *plain* ring tin. If the tin is not used for other cakes there is no need to grease it, but if it is used for many kinds of cakes, grease very lightly with a little olive oil. Put in the cake mixture, then tap the tin very sharply to get rid of any air bubbles, which would cause the cake to break when cooked. Bake the cake in an 8–9-inch ring tin for just about 1 hour in the centre of a slow oven, 300°F., Gas Mark 2, until firm to the touch. Do not attempt to turn the cake out of the tin at once: invert the tin on to a wire cooling tray, and allow the cake to drop out as it cools. Although this is often served as a plain cake, it is delicious coated with American frosting. This cake should be eaten within 1–2 days.

Frosted Angel cake

ingredients as Angel cake
above

American frosting
made with 8 oz. sugar
etc., as page 36

Make the Angel cake, often called Angel food cake in America. Cook and allow this to become quite cold before icing it. Prepare the American frosting as page 36. Lift the cake on to a board or plate. Spread the frosting quickly all over the cake. The 8 oz. sugar, etc., does not give a very thick layer, but the cake itself is sweet and therefore you do not use too much icing. Pages 32 and 33 give other suggestions for flavouring the cake, and choosing various icings for this.

Harlequin Angel cake

Make the Angel cake, recipe on left, put two-thirds of the mixture into 2 separate basins. Do this very gently, so that the light texture is not spoiled. Tint one-third a pale pink with a few drops of cochineal. Fold 2 teaspoons of well sieved cocoa into the other third with 1 tea-spoon water, to ensure a sufficiently soft texture. Put spoonfuls of the white, pink and chocolate mixtures into the tin. Bake as the Angel cake. Invert the tin over a wire cooling tray, so the cake will drop out. When cold, coat with American frosting, made with 8 oz. sugar etc., as page 36, or if preferred, flavour the frosting with chocolate, as the recipe on the same page.

Frosted Angel cakes keep a little longer than the plain one, on the left.

Coffee walnut layer cake

6 oz. butter or margarine
6–8 oz. castor sugar
4 large eggs
6 oz. flour (with plain flour
use 1½ level teaspoons
baking powder)
2 teaspoons instant coffee
2 oz. ground walnuts*

filling and coating
American frosting made
with 8 oz. sugar, etc.,
as page 36

decoration
about 12 halved walnuts

* ground in a liquidiser, chopped or minced

Cream the butter or margarine and sugar until soft and light. The larger amount of sugar gives a lighter, as well as sweeter, cake. Gradually beat in the eggs, then fold in the flour, or flour and baking powder, sieved with the coffee, and the walnuts. To economise on eggs use 3 only and 2 tablespoons milk or weak liquid coffee. Put into a well greased and floured or lined 7–8-inch cake tin, and bake in the centre of a slow to very moderate oven, 300–325°F., Gas Mark 2–3, for approximately 1¼–1½ hours, until just firm to the touch. Turn out carefully and cool. Make the frosting as page 36. Split the cake to give three layers, and sandwich together with thin layers of frosting. Coat with the remainder of the frosting, decorate with halved walnuts. This cake keeps about 2 weeks if stored in an air-tight tin. If wished, 2–3 oz. finely chopped walnuts may be added to the frosting used to sandwich the layers together; do not chop these too finely.

American chocolate layer cake
Coffee cream roll
(see instructions on page 32)

Feathering

Coffee cream roll

ingredients as Swiss roll page 28
little castor sugar

filling and coating
2 oz. butter or margarine
10 oz. sieved icing sugar

1 tablespoon instant coffee powder
2–3 tablespoons evaporated milk

decoration
1–2 oz. plain chocolate

Make the Swiss roll and bake as recipe page 28. Turn out when cooked on to sugared paper, roll round the paper and allow to cool. Cream the butter, icing sugar and coffee powder together, and gradually stir in the evaporated milk. Add sufficient to give a soft spreading consistency. Unroll the sponge carefully, spread with half the mixture and re-roll. Coat the cake with the rest of the mixture and mark with a small knife as shown in the picture. Meanwhile melt the chocolate as page 43; take care this does not become too hot otherwise it will lose its shine. Pour the chocolate on to a flat tin or slab to give a thin coating. Allow to cool, then mark into triangles. When firm press into the icing. This keeps several days. (Illustrated on page 31.)

1 FEATHERING is one of the most effective and simple forms of decoration. Coat the top of the cake with a layer of glacé icing, see pages 10–12. Make sure you have some left over, and tint this a different colour, or flavour and tint with cocoa or chocolate or coffee. Either pipe lines with a writing pipe, or make these by dipping a plain skewer in icing and 'drawing' the lines on the WET ground work.

American chocolate layer cake

2 oz. plain chocolate
4 oz. margarine
½ teaspoon vanilla essence
4 oz. flour (preferably plain with ½ teaspoon baking powder)
6 oz. castor sugar
2 oz. chopped walnuts
2 eggs

filling and coating
8 tablespoons water
1 lb. granulated sugar
2 egg whites
pinch cream of tartar
few walnuts

Melt the chocolate, margarine and essence in a good sized basin over hot water, cool. Add the sieved flour or flour and baking powder, the sugar, chopped nuts and the beaten eggs. Put into a 2 lb. loaf tin, lined with greased greaseproof paper, and bake for approximately 50 minutes in the centre of a very moderate oven, 325–350°F., Gas Mark 3–4. Turn out and cool, then cut into three layers. Make the American frosting as pages 36 and 37. Sandwich the layers together and coat the cake with the icing. Mark as in the picture, with a small knife. Press halved walnuts on top. This cake is also good with pecan or hazel nuts. It keeps for some days in an airtight tin. (Illustrated on page 31.)

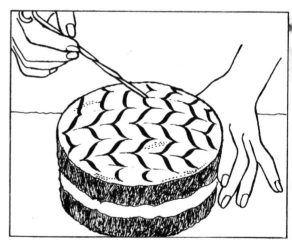

2 Take a clean skewer or use the back of a knife. 'Drag' the wet icing lines towards you at regular intervals. Next draw the skewer, or back of the knife, away from you, as shown in the picture, so you have the feathered effect. This decoration is equally suitable for small cakes or the top of biscuits.

Sponge fancies

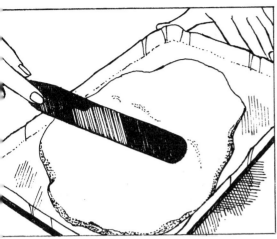

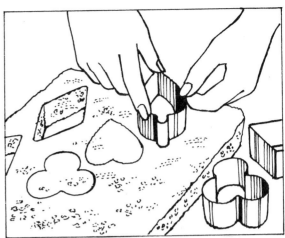

1 Choose either the whisked sponge on page 26, or the Victoria sponge recipe on page 6. Make the cake and put into a Swiss roll tin, lined with greased greaseproof paper. Let the paper stand up round the sides of the tin to support the cake as it cooks. Bake for the same time as given in either recipe for baking in 2 shallow tins, until firm to the touch.

2 Turn out the cake on to a wire cooling tray, and when cold remove the paper. Put on to a pastry board and cut into small shapes with a pastry cutter or sharp knife. Spread or brush the cakes with warmed sieved jam before icing, to give a moist texture and prevent the crumbs spoiling the icing.

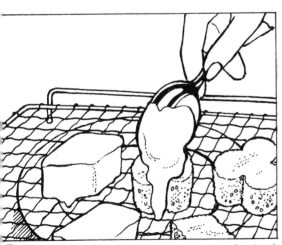

3 While these can be coated with soft glacé icing, made as pages 10–12, a flowing fondant icing, pages 34 and 35, gives a very smooth coating. Prepare the icing, then arrange the cakes on a wire cooling tray with a flat plate or dish underneath. Spoon the icing over the cakes, gather up any 'drips', reheat and use. Decorate with tiny pieces of cherry, angelica, etc., or with feathering, as the previous page.

4 The cakes may be made more interesting by spreading with a thick layer of butter icing, pages 13–15, or arranging small rolls of marzipan, page 38, on top of each cake before coating with icing. By coating the cakes with icing, the mixture made with Victoria sandwich would keep about a week, and with the true sponge for about 3 days.

Boiled Icings

I have grouped the boiled icings under the less simple types on page 9, as you *must* heat the sugar and water to the correct temperature. If insufficiently heated the icing will not set. If over-cooked it then becomes like a sweetmeat and the icing is spoiled, for it will be the wrong consistency.

The most usual and useful of boiled icings is a fondant. It is sometimes possible to buy this ready-made and you just need to handle it to make it pliable, or moisten it with a little sugar syrup as page 35, stage 4, recipe on the right. If you wish to make fondant at home the directions are on the right, or step-by-step on page 35, followed by those for American frosting. The difference between these two icings is that fondant does not use egg whites and is therefore a less light mixture. Use it for coating, as a filling, or for moulding. American frosting is used as a coating or filling. It is not sufficiently firm to handle for moulding. Fondant icing keeps well, so it is worthwhile making in bulk; it can be reheated, see page 35. American frosting keeps *on* the cake, but cannot be stored, so make just the right quantity.

Other interesting boiled icings in this book are the caramel coating, page 70, the very delicious fudge icing, page 68, and a marshmallow frosting, page 74.

Fondant

12 tablespoons water pinch cream of tartar
1 lb. granulated sugar

Put the water and sugar into a strong saucepan stir over a low heat until the sugar dissolve Add cream of tartar, boil steadily until the mixture reaches the 'soft ball' stage (explained o opposite page) or comes to 238°F. for a so fondant, or 240°F. for moulding. Beat unt mixture turns cloudy; use as step-by-ste directions on page 35. Store any left as stage on the same page.

Quantities needed

It is difficult to state amount needed for mould ing, so make plenty and store any left.

To give a flowing coating (very thin) over 6-inch cake, use 3 tablespoons water and 4 oz sugar with a pinch of cream of tartar. Allow double the amount for a thin layer over top an sides of a 6-inch cake (depth about 2 inches) or for a thick layer (moulded if required) over th top of a 6–7-inch cake. Other sizes use amount in proportion; and very much the same a American frosting, page 36.

Flavourings for fondant

The flavourings used in fondant are much th same as those given on page 36 for America frosting. Remember these are calculated o 8 oz. sugar, so if you are making a larger quan tity of fondant to store, increase accordingly It is often better to make up the plain fondan in bulk, then flavour as and when needed.

For a flowing fondant you can soften the icing with fruit juice. Work cocoa, or melted choco late, or coffee into the fondant.

SUGAR SYRUP is mentioned for softening fondant, or instead of water in mixing glace icing, page 12. To make this, heat $\frac{1}{4}$ pint wate and 8 oz. granulated sugar to 220°F. Store in screw-topped jar; use as required.

Using fondant icing

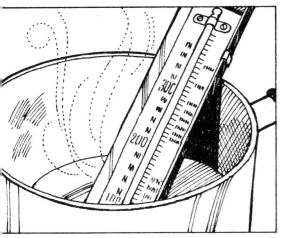

1 Since fondant icing keeps for some time it is worth making quite an amount, even if you do not use it all at once. Put 12 tablespoons water and 1 lb. granulated sugar into a strong pan. Stir over a low heat until the sugar dissolves, add a pinch of cream of tartar, then boil steadily until the mixture reaches a 'soft ball' stage, this is explained on page 36, or 238°F.–240°F.

2 Beat until the mixture turns cloudy. If you wish to mould the icing, see stage 3. If you wish to use the icing at once, add about 1 tablespoon warm water or sugar syrup, page 34, to the cloudy mixture, and blend well. You need to produce a texture that can be used as a filling or a smooth coating, see picture above, so if necessary add more liquid. Page 34 gives quantities to use for various sized cakes.

3 To mould fondant icing, turn from the pan when cloudy (do not add extra water) on to a board. Cool enough to handle, then roll out like marzipan. If the icing seems a little soft, work in enough sieved icing sugar to give a firm texture. Use as marzipan to coat a cake, or mould flowers, etc., as page 56.

4 Store any icing left in a polythene bag, or really airtight tin. To use again, put into a basin and add a little warm water or sugar syrup, see page 34. The icing can then be made into just the texture required. Blend well if a soft texture, and use as stage 2, or knead well and use as stage 3.

American frosting

This icing has many advantages, for it is sufficiently soft and delicate to coat light sponge cakes, yet it makes an excellent alternative over marzipan (or by itself) as a coating for Christmas cakes. Many people dislike both marzipan and the rather hard Royal icing. This is when you should choose American frosting. It is quite hard on the outside after storing a while, but keeps a soft texture in the centre. It also cuts very well.

Like any mixture that must be boiled to a given temperature, great care should be taken that you do not exceed this. If using a sugar thermometer, allow the temperature of the mixture to reach 238°F. if you like a softer frosting, or 240°F. for a slightly firmer texture.

If you *do not* possess a sugar thermometer then have a basin of cold water beside the cooker. *Test frequently* by dropping a little of the syrup into the water. When the mixture is sufficiently firm to roll into a soft ball, the icing is ready. *Always take the pan off the cooker* or turn off the heat as you test, so the sugar and water do not continue boiling.

It is important to beat the mixture until cloudy *in the pan*, then to pour as quickly as possible on to the stiffly beaten egg white or whites, see page 37, stages 2 and 3.

Quantities needed

American frosting may be spread very thinly, or piled into a generous layer to stand in peaks on the cake, so there is some variation in the size of the cakes that may be covered with a given amount of icing.

To coat top of a 6 or 7-inch cake, use basic recipe with 8 oz. sugar, etc. Allow double this amount to coat top and sides of the cake (depth about 3 inches) and you may have enough for a thin layer of filling. To coat top of an 8 or 9-inch cake, use 1 lb. sugar, etc., or for a thin layer, only 12 oz. sugar, etc., (with 1½ egg whites). To coat a 10 or 11-inch cake, use 1 lb. sugar, etc., for a thin layer, but 1½ lb. sugar, etc., for a really generous topping.

American frosting

4 tablespoons water	1 egg white
8 oz. granulated sugar	pinch cream of tartar

Put the water and sugar into a strong saucepan Stir over a low heat until the sugar dissolves Boil steadily until the mixture reaches the 'soft ball' stage, i.e. 238°F. to 240°F., see column or left. While the syrup is boiling, whisk the egg white until stiff. Beat the syrup until cloudy Pour the syrup steadily on to the egg white, see next page, stages 2 and 3. Add the cream o tartar, and continue beating until the mixture stands up in peaks. Use at once as a filling or fo coating the cake, see next page. If using American frosting for a Christmas cake, sweep up in peaks as suggested for Royal icing or page 47. This icing will keep on cakes for some weeks in perfect condition, but cannot be used for piping.

Flavourings for frosting

The amounts below are for 8 oz. sugar, etc.

Almond, Vanilla, etc: for various sponges etc. Add up to 1 teaspoon flavouring essence to the water and sugar before cooking.

Chocolate: for plain, coffee or chocolate cakes. Blend 1 level tablespoon sieved cocoa or 2 tablespoons chocolate powder, with the icing when it reaches 238°F.–240°F.

Coffee: for plain, coffee or chocolate cakes Use strong coffee in place of water in the recipe

Coconut: for plain, coconut or most flavoured cakes. Add 3 oz. desiccated or shredded well drained fresh coconut to the icing when it reaches 238°F.–240°F.

Fruit: for most cakes. Use fresh orange or canned pineapple juice in place of water, or half fresh lemon or grapefruit juice and half water. Very finely grated fruit rind may be added before cooking.

There are other variations which are given in individual recipes.

Using American frosting

1 There are several recipes for this icing, but the following proportions produce a frosting that reaches the right temperature quickly. Put 4 tablespoons water and 8 oz. granulated sugar into a strong saucepan. Stir over a low heat until the sugar dissolves. Boil steadily until the mixture reaches a 'soft ball' stage, or 238°F.–240°F., this is explained on page 36.

2 While the syrup is boiling, beat 1 egg white in a strong basin until very stiff. Have the cake ready for icing, since this frosting sets very quickly. You can use an electric mixer but *make sure the bowl will not crack from hot syrup*. Beat the syrup in the pan until it begins to turn cloudy, *do not leave after this*, but continue to stage 3 at once.

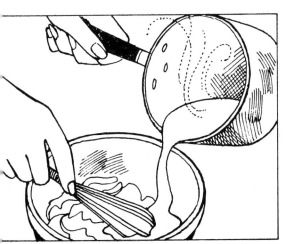

3 Pour the syrup from the pan steadily on to the stiffly beaten egg white, whisking all the time. It is, therefore, a good idea to pour with the saucepan in your left hand and whisk with your right hand. When all the syrup is added, put in a pinch of cream of tartar. Continue whisking until the mixture stands up in peaks, then add any flavouring, see page 36, and colouring.

4 Spread over the top, or top and sides, or as a filling and topping on the cake. Page 36 gives quantities to use for various sized cakes. Spread a filling flat, but 'swirl' the topping into peaks. Decorate, if wished, with cherries, nuts, etc. Leave to become quite cold.

Marzipan

This very delicious icing is not only a perfect coating for cakes, but a very adaptable mixture that can be moulded or rolled out like pastry, or baked, as in a Simnel cake.

If the cake is not a perfect shape then use the marzipan to improve upon this. Fill in any small cracks in the cake with a little marzipan, and take time to make the marzipan coating as perfect as possible, for this will give you an excellent base for whichever icing you choose

The recipe on the right gives the proportions for the best known marzipan, but try the variations sometimes, for a change. The economical recipes provide a considerably cheaper coating.

Mention is made below of not over-handling marzipan. This is because the more it is kneaded and handled the greater the chance of the almond oil 'seeping-out' from the ground almonds and discolouring the icing.

There are several ways in which you can prevent the oil spoiling the icing:

a) brush the marzipan with egg white before putting on the top icing. Let the egg white dry-out, this takes about 15 minutes, and it will form a protective covering between the marzipan and the icing.

b) allow the marzipan itself to dry-out for 48 hours before putting on the icing. This has long been recommended advice; personally I dislike it, for the marzipan tends to become dry and hard. I follow points a) and c).

c) *handle the marzipan as quickly and deftly* as possible, so that it does not become over-kneaded and oily. This takes practice, but it means you can then coat the cake with its glaze of sieved jam or egg white, put on the marzipan, follow point a) and then put on the icing, or the first coat of icing, *immediately*. As a result the marzipan is always soft but does not spoil the icing.

Basic marzipan

4 oz. ground almonds	1 egg yolk
2 oz. icing sugar	
2 oz. castor sugar	**to roll out**
few drops almond essence	little castor sugar

Put the ground almonds into a mixing bowl add the sieved icing sugar, castor sugar and essence. Mix lightly, stir in the egg yolk. This should give sufficient moisture to bind the ingredients together without much handling but the softness of ground almonds and size of egg yolks vary a little. If the marzipan seems too dry, add part of a second egg yolk, a little egg white, or orange flower water. Form into a ball put on to a sugared board and roll to size required.

Note. You may also bind the marzipan with whole eggs; this may be more economical when making a large quantity. You can use all egg white instead of yolk; this tends to give a less moist marzipan. In most cases though, it is better to use the yolks for the marzipan, and save the whites for Royal icing or American frosting.

Quantities needed

The simplest way to calculate the total amount of marzipan required for large rich fruit cakes is to use just about half the total weight of the cake. However, here are some simple calculations to help.

To coat top of an 8-inch round or 7-inch square cake, use minimum of 4 oz. ground almonds, etc., as recipe above. Allow double this amount to coat top and sides of the cake (depth about $2\frac{1}{2}$ inches), although in fact one generally uses just over half the marzipan for the sides.

To coat top of a 9-inch round or 8-inch square cake, use minimum of 6 oz. ground almonds, etc. To coat top of a 10-inch round or 9-inch square cake, use 8 oz. ground almonds, etc. Make more in proportion if you also wish to coat sides.

Flavourings for marzipan

The strong almond flavour of marzipan makes other flavouring unnecessary, except in exceptional cases, see individual recipes.

Economical marzipan

Follow directions for the basic marzipan, but use only 2 oz. ground almonds, 4 oz. sieved icing sugar, 2 oz. castor sugar. Bind with the essence, egg yolk and squeeze lemon juice.

Rich marzipan

Follow directions for marzipan, but use only part of an egg yolk and a little brandy to bind.

Cooked marzipan

As mentioned on page 8, cooked marzipan is not often made at home since the other recipe is so simple, but this is a very firm icing and if making fondant you can use part as a basis for marzipan, the rest for a coating. Make fondant as page 34, with 12 tablespoons water, 1 lb. granulated sugar and a pinch cream of tartar. *If using all of this for marzipan,* weigh out 12 oz. ground almonds.

Boil the fondant to 240°F. (a soft ball stage), beat until slightly cloudy in the pan, then add the ground almonds, a few drops almond essence and 2 lightly whisked egg whites. Heat gently for about 2–3 minutes, then cool and handle as marzipan. This is particularly good for moulding, and will, as you see, use a smaller quantity of the rather expensive ground almonds. Obviously, if using a smaller amount of fondant, then calculate ground almonds and egg whites in proportion.

Note. To economise still further, use 4 oz. fine semolina and 8 oz. ground almonds in place of 12 oz. ground almonds.

Using ready-made marzipan

This varies in both colour and flavour. The pale marzipan is generally a cooked variety, rather as the recipe above. The bright golden is more like the uncooked basic recipe, but often sweeter, as more sugar and less ground almonds are used. When calculating weight to buy, you need 1 lb. bought marzipan instead of a recipe that states 8 oz. ground almonds, etc.

Simnel cake

6 oz. butter or margarine
6 oz. moist brown sugar
2 teaspoons golden syrup
3 large eggs
8 oz. flour (preferably plain with 1 level teaspoon baking powder)
½–1 teaspoon powdered cinnamon
½–1 teaspoon mixed spice
1½ tablespoons milk
1 lb. dried fruit

2 oz. chopped blanched almonds
2 oz. halved glacé cherries

filling and topping
marzipan * made with 12 oz. ground almonds, etc., page 38
little castor sugar
1 tablespoon apricot jam
little egg white

Cream the butter or margarine, sugar and golden syrup until soft and light. Add the well beaten eggs gradually. Sieve the flour and baking powder with the spices and fold into the creamed mixture, add the milk, fruit, almonds and quartered cherries. Make the marzipan* — this amount gives a most generous topping; if you want a plainer one then make marzipan with only 8 oz. ground almonds, etc. Take about one-third of the marzipan and roll it out on a sugared board to 8 inches in diameter, or the size of the cake tin. Line the cake tin with greased greaseproof paper. Put in half the cake mixture, then the round of marzipan. Cover with the rest of the cake mixture, smooth quite flat on top.

Bake in the centre of a very moderate oven, 325–350°F., Gas Mark 3–4, for about 45 minutes only, then lower the heat to slow, approximately 300°F., Gas Mark 2, for a further 1¾ hours. The 'damp' marzipan in the centre of the cake delays cooking quite a lot, and it is therefore very important to lower the heat in plenty of time, so the cake does not become over-brown on the outside before it is cooked in the centre. The slightly hotter oven at the beginning of cooking sets the outside and ensures a pleasantly moist cake. Test carefully by seeing if it is firm on top and shrunk away from the sides of the tin. Cool slightly before turning out of tin. When cool, brush the top of the cake with the apricot jam. Roll out half remaining marzipan, press on top of the cake.

Use the rest to make balls around the edge of the cake, as the picture on page 41, stage 6. Brush with egg white. Brown under a grill, set to a very low heat, or for 10–15 minutes in a very moderate oven.

If wished, put a little icing in the centre of the cake before decorating with chickens, or other Easter decorations. Keeps some weeks.

Using marzipan

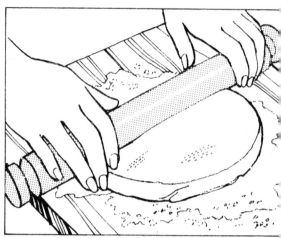

1 While there are several recipes for marzipan, or almond paste, the most usual is to blend 4 oz. ground almonds with 2 oz. sieved icing sugar, 2 oz. castor sugar, a few drops of almond or ratafia essence, and an egg yolk. Quantities needed to coat various sized cakes are shown on page 38. Knead lightly and carefully. Brush the cake to be coated with egg white, or sieved apricot jam.

2 Put the marzipan on a sugared board, roll out to size and thickness required. One way to coat the cake is shown above, i.e. to make one piece sufficiently large to put over the cake. Mould this gently with your hands to adhere to the cake, *do not over-handle*, see reasons on page 38. If preferred, use the method of coating shown in stages 3 and 4.

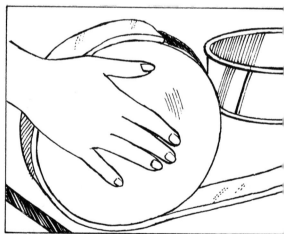

3 Use just under half the marzipan to coat the top of the cake. Roll this out to a round exactly the same size as the cake, use the cake tin as a guide. There are two ways of putting this on to the cake, a) press on the cake, or b) turn the cake upside down on to the marzipan and press firmly.

4 Make a band of marzipan the depth of the cake, use the cake tin as a guide for the correct size, or measure with a ruler. Try and make one band the length of the circumference of the cake; the fewer the joins, the neater the cake. Lay the cake on the strip of marzipan, and roll slowly and firmly so this sticks to the cake.

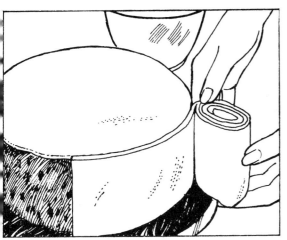

5 Stages 3 and 4 are the more usual way of putting marzipan on to a cake, you may prefer to put the side band on *before* the top round. Press the side band and top round together, then flatten with a rolling pin. Use this in an upright position for the sides of the cake, or roll with a jam jar. The neater the marzipan, the better the base for the icing. Picture shows an alternative method of putting the side band on.

6 Marzipan may be moulded into flowers, as fondant and other moulding icings, see page 56, or any other shapes desired. The picture above though shows marzipan uncoated, as the icing on a Simnel cake, recipe page 39.

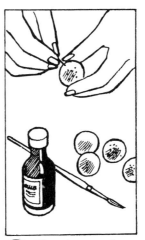

7 Either tint the marzipan yellow, or form into *banana* shapes first and brush with yellow colouring. Mark tiny brown streaks with liquid coffee on the tip of a brush or use melted chocolate.

8 To make an *apple* tint one side of the little balls with green, then the other with a red colouring. Flatten slightly to an apple shape, press a clove into the base as the flower bud.

9 Tint the marzipan an even orange colouring, or form the balls then brush with orange colouring, prick gently with a pin to give the pitted look of an *orange*.

10 *Pears* are made as apples, form the shape first then continue as stage 8. Roll all fruits gently in castor sugar to dry out.

Battenburg

Apple marzipan tarts

4 oz. short crust pastry
about ½ pint *very thick*
   sweetened apple purée

marzipan with 4 oz. ground
   almonds, etc.
2 oz. plain chocolate

Roll out the pastry thinly and line 12 patty tins. Bake above the centre of a hot oven, 425–450°F., Gas Mark 6–7, for about 10 minutes until golden brown. Cool, fill with the apple purée. Roll out the marzipan and cut into 12 rounds to fit over the apple. Melt the chocolate and place a round in the centre of the marzipan 'lid'. Eat when fresh.

Battenburg cake

Victoria sponge with
   3 eggs, etc., page 16
few drops cochineal or
   ½ oz. cocoa
3 tablespoons sieved jam

marzipan with 8 oz.
   ground almonds, etc.,
   page 38
little castor sugar
few glacé cherries
angelica

Make the sponge mixture as page 16, put half into a basin and tint with the cochineal. If preferred blend in the sieved cocoa, and about 1 dessertspoon water, to give the soft consistency again. Line a small Swiss roll tin with greased greaseproof paper, but let it stand up well above the sides of the tin to support the cake as it rises. Make a stiff band of greaseproof paper the width of the tin, grease on both sides. Put the white cake mixture into half the tin, add the paper band, then put the pink or chocolate mixture at the other end of the tin. Bake for approximately 20–25 minutes above the centre of a moderate oven, 350–375°F., Gas Mark 4–5, until firm to the touch. Turn out and cool. Cut into 4 strips, coat sides of one pink or chocolate, and one plain strip, with warmed jam. Now coat the top of these and place a pink or chocolate strip on the plain one, and a plain strip on the coloured one. Coat joins and top of the cake with jam. Roll out the marzipan on a well sugared board to an oblong sufficiently wide and long to cover the cake. Make sure it is neither too sticky, nor over-hard so that it breaks when lifted round the cake. Slip a fish slice under the cake and turn it upside down (so the jam-coated top now becomes the bottom) and place it in the centre of the marzipan. Continue as step-by-step directions, right. This cake, if well wrapped, keeps for 1–2 weeks; it freezes well.

1 Brush the sides and the top of the cake (originally the bottom) with jam, then lift the marzipan up to cover the cake. Seal the edges well, and press the marzipan firmly so it will not break away from the cake.

2 Turn the cake upside down again, so the join in the marzipan is now at the bottom. Pinch the edges of the marzipan to give an attractive fluted design. Score the top of the marzipan with a knife to give a criss-cross design. Press the glacé cherries and leaves of angelica into position, or decorate with chocolate leaves as the picture opposite, stage 4.

Using chocolate

1 Break the chocolate into pieces. Choose plain or cooking chocolate, see page 69. Put into the top of a double saucepan or basin, standing over a pan of water. Allow the water to become hot but not to boil, do NOT stir as the chocolate melts. Remove, cool, stir and add a few drops olive oil, glycerine or a tiny knob of butter, to keep the shine. Pour over the cake or use as the recipes, e.g. Chocolate cream sponge, page 28, and Chocolate rum gâteau, page 69.

2 Melted chocolate may be used for *piping lines and scrolls*, etc. Decide on the design, if necessary mark this lightly on waxed paper (this is better than greaseproof paper). Use a writing pipe, fill the bag or syringe with the liquid, but fairly cool, chocolate. Pipe into the required design. If piping on paper, allow to become hard, remove carefully from paper; store in a tin.

3 *To make chocolate curls*, sometimes called Chocolate Caraque, melt the chocolate as stage 1, then pour on to a marble slab or flat tin. Allow to set lightly then run a sharp pliable knife along the chocolate, do this slowly and carefully, making curls of chocolate. Leave these until very hard, then use as decorations on cakes, see page 69.

4 Use melted chocolate to make *leaf designs*, e.g. holly, rose, or other fairly simple leaves. Wash and dry the real leaves. Melt the chocolate as stage 1, then brush the under-side of each leaf (this is better than the shiny top surface) with a good layer of the melted chocolate. Leave to set, remove with the tip of a knife. Store in a tin.

Royal Icing

This very popular icing is used on many rich cakes; for birthdays, for wedding and Christmas cakes. It is a perfect icing for piping, but is too brittle for moulding.

One of the drawbacks about Royal icing is that it is inclined to become very hard, and some people dislike this. In the next column you will find hints on keeping it softer, either by using olive oil, or glycerine, and on making a modified Royal icing with a mixture of water and egg whites.

I have not discussed flavourings for Royal icing as lemon juice is generally chosen; naturally you can flavour the icing if you wish, but most people prefer to use other kinds of icings if they want a strong taste.

When icing special cakes, such as a wedding or birthday cake, you will achieve a better finish with two thinner coats rather than a single thick one. Allow the first coat to dry thoroughly before applying the second.

To make Royal icing

2 egg whites   1 tablespoon lemon juice
1 lb. sieved icing sugar

Whisk the egg whites lightly, do not over-beat. Gradually add the icing sugar, which must be very well sieved. Tiny lumps do NOT come out with mixing, and this is likely to impede piping and spoil the perfect surface of the cake. Add the lemon juice, and continue to beat until the icing is very white and stands up in peaks. Often this icing is made either too stiff or over-beaten for *coating* a cake. The peaks should *not* be too sharp and upright for coating the cake, they should be soft, rather like lightly whipped cream. For *piping* though, make sure the icing is beaten enough to give you firm-looking upright peaks – do not add more sugar – achieve this with beating.

If using an electric mixer take care you do not over-beat. Choose a low speed and allow the mixer to run *only* until the right consistency is reached. Over-beating gives air bubbles in the icing which are almost impossible to remove.

If you do not wish the icing to become too hard, use up to 1 teaspoon glycerine, or a few drops olive oil, or use the icing below.

Modified Royal icing

Use the method of mixing above, but omit 1 egg white and use a little warm water instead. For coating you will probably need about 2–3 tablespoonfuls; for simple line piping barely 2 tablespoonfuls.

This icing is not good for piping flowers, etc.

Quantities needed

This depends upon whether you intend to use one or two coats on a cake. For one coat only (this does not include much piping) on the top of a 7-inch cake, use 8 oz. icing sugar, etc. Allow at least double this amount for top and sides of the cake.

If you wish to put a thick icing on a 7-inch Christmas cake, or two coats plus quite elaborate piping, you need about 2 lb. icing.

Using Royal icing

1 Beat 2 egg whites lightly, do not over-beat. Add 1 lb. sieved icing sugar gradually, 1 tablespoon lemon juice, and glycerine if wished, see page 44. Stir together, then beat hard until a smooth texture and white in colour. Page 44 discusses the use of an electric mixer.

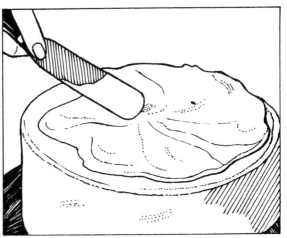

2 When the icing is exactly the right consistency (page 44 tells you more about this and the quantities needed to cover cakes) spoon all the icing on to the top of the cake, then gradually work from the centre to the sides, see stage 3.
Note. If the icing is made any time before being needed, cover the bowl with a damp cloth so that it does not harden.

3 Spread the icing over the sides of the cake to give an even coating, make sure the sides are completely covered before you try and neaten these.

4 Neaten the top of the cake with long sweeping movements, holding the edge of the knife or ruler against the icing. Neaten the sides with gentle vertical movements with the palette knife against the icing. Rotate the turntable as you do this.

Christmas Cakes

Christmas cakes may be iced elaborately and decorated with piping, or they can be very effective with the simple 'snow' effect shown on the opposite page. If you wish to use this form of decoration then choose either American frosting, pages 36 and 37, and boil the mixture to 240°F., so that you make it sufficiently firm to hold the 'peaks', or use Royal icing, described on pages 44 and 45.

If, on the other hand, you prefer a smooth coating you may still use Royal icing, or choose fondant, pages 34 and 35, or plastic icing, shown on pages 53 and 54.

In order to enjoy a rich Christmas cake (as recipe right) at its best, bake the cake at least a month beforehand, and store it in an airtight tin so that it matures in flavour. Coat and decorate about a week before Christmas. If you dislike marzipan, then cover the cake with an extra layer of icing instead. Allow this to harden and cover with one or two more coats. This ensures that the grease from the cake will not spoil the colour of the icing.

For a smaller and less rich cake, use the Simnel cake recipe on page 39. Omit the marzipan through the centre.

Rich dark Christmas Cake

10 oz. butter or table margarine	½ teaspoon grated nutmeg
10 oz. moist brown sugar	1 lb. currants*
1 level tablespoon black treacle or golden syrup	12 oz. sultanas*
5 large eggs	8 oz. seedless raisins*
12 oz. flour, preferably plain	4 oz. candied peel
½ teaspoon mixed spice	4 oz. glacé cherries
	2 oz. ground almonds
	2 tablespoons brandy or sherry or lemon juice

* if fruit is washed, dry at room temperature for 48 hours

Cream the butter or margarine, sugar and treacle or syrup. Gradually beat in the eggs, then add the flour, sieved with the spices. Do not over beat this mixture, for that could cause the fruit to sink in the cake. Mix the dried fruit with the chopped peel and quartered cherries, add to the cake mixture with the ground almonds, brandy or sherry or lemon juice. Mix very well. Put into a prepared tin, see page 58, choose an 8-inch square tin with minimum depth of 3 inches, or a 9–10-inch round tin. Smooth the mixture flat on top and press gently with damp knuckles; this helps to keep the cake from cracking, and quite level as it cooks, although the moist mixture and plain flour help to ensure this. Bake for approximately 4 hours in the case of an 8 or 9-inch cake, and about 3½ hours for a 10-inch cake. Set the oven at very moderate, 325–350°F., Gas Mark 3, for the first 1¼ hours, until the cake is very pale-coloured and beginning to set. After this, lower the heat to slow, 275–300°F., Gas Mark 1–2, for the remainder of the time.

To test a rich cake like this, press firmly on top and if no impression is left by your finger then see if the cake has shrunk slightly from the sides of the tin. If so, remove from the oven and listen carefully. An uncooked rich fruit cake makes a faint 'humming' noise. If cooked there is no sound. Cool in the tin, then turn out very carefully. Do not turn out when hot, as the weight of the fruit could cause the cake to break.

To give a moist texture and real flavour of brandy or sherry to the cake, prick after baking when cold, and pour over a little sherry or brandy. Do this at weekly intervals.

To decorate Christmas cakes

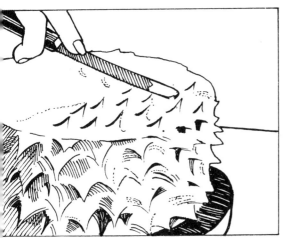

1 *Snow effect.* Coat the cake with marzipan as pages 38–41, then with a thick layer of Royal icing, pages 44 and 45. Sweep the icing into peaks while still soft. Use the tip of a knife as shown in the picture above.

If using American frosting, pages 36 and 37, swirl the icing into peaks as you cover the cake.

2 Complete the cake with tiny figures, and arrange small sprigs of holly round the sides of the cake. A small round of aluminium foil can be put on top of the cake to look like a miniature lake, with tiny figures 'skating' on this.

3 This Christmas cake shows a compromise between a smooth coating and the 'snow' effect. Coat the cake with marzipan, as pages 38–41, then with a smooth coating of Royal icing, pages 44 and 45, or fondant, pages 34 and 35, or plastic icing, pages 53 to 54. Put a small 'snow' scene at one side of the cake with appropriate figures. Write Christmas greetings in a bright red icing, see page 48 on piping.

4 This is a more ambitious Christmas cake. Coat with marzipan, as pages 38–41, then with a layer of plastic icing, pages 53 to 54. Decorate with roses made with plastic icing and Christmas greetings in bright coloured Royal icing. The piping round the bottom edge of the cake is also made with Royal icing.

Piping

Do not be disappointed if your first efforts at piping are not as perfect as you would wish. It takes both time and practice to achieve expertise. There are certain points that help when piping.

The butter or Royal icing must be the right consistency, for too stiff a mixture makes it difficult to force the icing through the bag, or syringe, and the icing pipe. Too soft an icing fails to hold the piped shape. Pages 13–15, and 44–45, give details of correct proportions for the icings.

The angle at which you hold the syringe or bag and pipe is all important. For writing, or a flowing design, hold at the angle you would a pen. For an upright design (star, rose, etc.) hold the pipe at right angles to the surface of the cake.

The icing pipes can be fitted into material or paper bags, or a syringe. If using a nylon bag (the most usual material) or a syringe, buy icing pipes with a rim that fits a screw attachment. This is not necessary when putting the pipe into a paper bag, although you *can* use a pipe with a rim.

First steps to piping

Make quite certain that the coating on the cake is firm before beginning to pipe on this. If you have made one batch of butter or Royal icing for both coating and piping, always cover the basin containing the surplus icing for piping with damp paper, or a damp cloth, so it does not dry out and become too hard to use.

Work out the design on a piece of paper the same size and shape as the cake. The icing rings, shown on page 5, will help to make this symmetrical. Lay the paper design on the cake and 'prick out' the same pattern with the tip of a fine needle. Remove the paper and you then have a perfect guide from the tiny holes on the cake.

Make up the paper bags if using these; do make several so you can change to a new one without delay, see the opposite page.

Insert the pipe into the bag, or screw it firmly on to the attachment in a nylon bag, or at the base of a syringe.

Check the consistency of the icing before putting into the bag, or syringe, and after filling these. Pipe one or two stars or lines on to a pastry board or tin, to make quite certain the icing is perfect. For writing, the icing must flow steadily to give unbroken letters.

If writing, it is a good idea to prick out the greeting with a fine needle, then to form the letters with a fine writing pipe. If too fine, allow the letters to dry then pipe again, either with the same pipe, which will raise the letters, or with a larger size or perhaps an even finer pipe in a darker or lighter shade.

If making stars, rosettes, etc., check on the size you wish these to be. The longer you apply gentle pressure to the top of the bag or syringe, the larger will be the star or rosette.

Never fill either bags or a syringe too full, otherwise the icing can 'ooze out' at the top. Most people find a paper bag gives 'greater control' over the icing.

Page 5 gives suggestions for the first few pipes to buy, but on page 50 you will find a larger selection of pipes, with an idea of the shapes they can form. On page 51 pipes are used to form flowers, and to give designs on icing nails.

Making and filling an icing bag

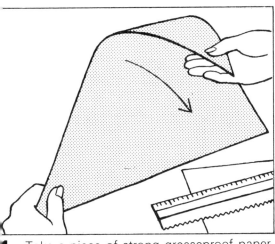

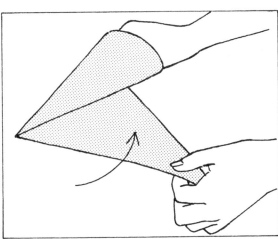

1 Take a piece of strong greaseproof paper, an ideal size is 10 inches square. Cut into two triangles. Take hold of the top right-hand corner and turn this so the point is folded between the thumb and forefinger of the right hand. Hold the left-hand corner firmly in the left hand.

2 Roll the right hand over until the point on the left corner is almost reached, then bring this point up to meet the others, see the picture above, so making a sharply pointed cone.

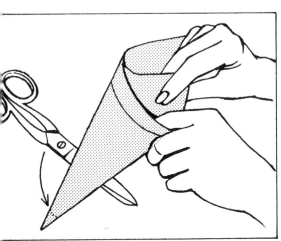

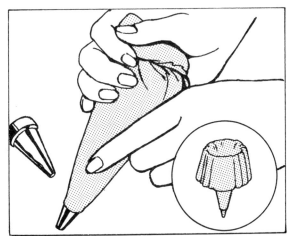

3 Secure the top of the cone by tucking in the edges firmly. Snip a very tiny piece from the base of the cone and put the pipe into the bag, make sure it is protruding properly and the paper cone fits round firmly. Half fill the bag with icing and fold the top paper over, so covering the icing and making the bag easy to hold. Apply gentle pressure to the top of the bag.

4 If using a nylon bag, screw the pipe on to the attachment in the base of this. Either hold the nylon bag in the left hand and fold back the material, or support the bag in a small jug or cup with the top material folded back. Half fill with the icing. Bring back the top material and press the icing gently through the pipe.

Selection of pipes and designs

Here are some of the most useful pipes available and the designs that can be made from them. Those shown are the rimmed type, suitable for screwing on, or inserting into, a bag. The rimless type have different numbers.

Happy

WISHES

Two-tier wedding cake with shell and rope edgings, and silver decorations

Piping flowers

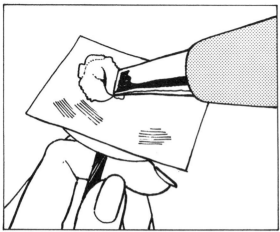

1 *Keep the Royal icing firm* for flowers. Several pipes make petals, above is No. 11 (screw type). Put a square of waxed paper on the icing nail, secure with icing. For a flat petal keep the hole in the pipe flat against the paper. Squeeze gently, guiding the icing from the centre to the outside, then back again. Break off, this makes the first petal. Continue to form the flower, turn the nail as you work.

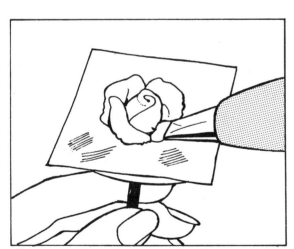

2 Pipes 36, 18, 43 all make roses. Make the centre of the rose by turning the icing round to form a cone. As you work rotate the icing nail. Now begin to form petals as the picture above, turning the nail all the time. If you have no icing nails, then grease cocktail sticks and form the flower round these. When hard the flowers may be removed and stored in a box. Tint by brushing lightly with culinary colours.

Piping trellis

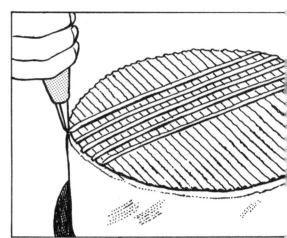

1 Trellis work may be piped directly on to the cake, as the picture above. *The Royal icing should flow steadily*, so check the consistency. Choose writing pipes 0–2 (screw type); a 00 is too fine and a 3 rather thick. Work out the design, see page 48, then pipe all the lines going in one direction. ALLOW THESE TO DRY, then pipe the next set of lines diagonally or at right angles across the first.

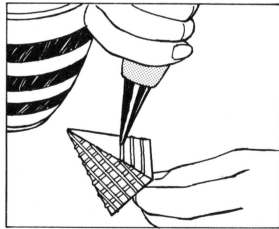

2 If you wish the trellis work to 'stand away' from the cake then pipe over a well polished or very lightly greased icing nail or patty tin. The type of icing nail required is called a 'net nail', but all shapes in patty tins may be used. Pipe as stage 1 above, over the nail, allow the first layer to harden before starting the second. When all the icing is very hard, gently remove the nail or patty tin.

Plastic Icings

The term plastic icing may not sound very appealing, but this particular coating is given this name, to differentiate between it and the cooked fondant on page 34. The most usual plastic icing contains liquid glucose, which generally has to be ordered from a chemist. If not obtainable, use the satin icing given on page 54, or the boiled fondant.

Although you can take some of the plastic icing made for coating and put it on one side to use for moulding, I find the second recipe, page 54, gives a better result. If any of the icing is left over, keep in a polythene bag; knead well before using again. This icing keeps for months.

This icing enables you to have gracefully rounded corners on a cake and to mould all flowers, etc., with great delicacy, indeed the petals can be made as thin as those on real flowers.

Plastic icing for coating

The quantities given below are sufficient to give a moderately thick coating on a 7-inch round cake, with a little left for moulding — if you do not wish to make a separate amount, using the slightly different recipe on page 54. As glucose is sticky to handle, I suggest you put the saucepan on to the scales and pour the glucose into the pan until the desired weight is obtained.

for coating	for rolling
$\frac{1}{2}$ oz. (1 tablespoon) powder gelatine	extra icing sugar sprinkling cornflour
2 oz. (3 tablespoons) water or lemon juice	
4 oz. liquid glucose	
3 teaspoons glycerine	
2 lb. sieved icing sugar	

Put the gelatine and water, or lemon juice, into a small container in a pan of boiling water. Leave until softened, then stir until dissolved. Tip into a large saucepan with the glucose and glycerine, and stir over a very low heat until well blended. Mix with the icing sugar; this can be done in the saucepan, or tip the gelatine, etc., into the icing sugar in a bowl. Mix very well with your hands, and knead until blended and smooth. If you wish to colour the icing it is best to add this to the gelatine, etc. Sprinkle a large pastry board with icing sugar and a very little cornflour (this is not tasted in the icing). Make sure the icing sugar is well sieved. Knead again until there are no cracks, then roll out until sufficiently large to cover the cake. Coat the cake with sieved jam, then with marzipan if wished. Brush the marzipan with a little egg white, allow to dry. When ready, lift the icing over a rolling pin and lower it carefully on to the cake. Remove the rolling pin and allow the icing to cover the cake. Mould to the shape of the cake, then cut away any surplus icing from the base of the cake.

Leave overnight, then pipe on the cake with Royal icing. The secret of a glossy shine on this plastic icing is to shake a little sieved icing sugar into the palms of your hands, and rub slowly and firmly over the cake until it has a very attractive shine. This icing never becomes over-hard.

Two recipes for plastic icing, both excellent for moulding, are given on page 54. The recipe for Satin icing is also given on page 54.

Quantities of plastic icing

While one can make plastic icing wafer-thin for moulding, I find I prefer a moderately thick layer for coating cakes; so all amounts are adequate for this. It is usual to coat the whole cake, but if you prefer to put a layer on the top only, use half or just under half quantities. The amounts given allow for moulding one large flower, figure, etc. — if you do not wish to make the slightly different icing below, see coating recipe page 53.

For top and sides of an 8-inch square or 9-inch round cake, use 3 lb. icing sugar and all other ingredients in proportion, i.e. half as much again as recipe page 53. For the top and sides of a 9-inch square or 10-inch round tin, allow double recipe on page 53. For the top and sides of a 10-inch square or 11-inch round cake, allow 5 lb. icing sugar, etc. *This becomes a very heavy quantity to handle* and I prefer to make 2 batches, then knead them together after they have become smooth. This icing keeps for months.

Plastic icing for moulding (1)

To make a good sized spray of flowers for one cake you will need 8 oz. icing sugar, etc.

1 teaspoon powder gelatine	2 teaspoons liquid glucose
½ tablespoon water or lemon juice	8 oz. sieved icing sugar colouring

Dissolve the gelatine in the small quantity of liquid as page 53. Heat with the glucose, and add the icing sugar and any colouring required. If making mixed flowers, it is a good idea to work in white icing and brush on the tint with a fine paint brush and culinary colourings. Knead very well, and to form any flowers take a small piece of the icing and press it with your fingers in the palm of your hand until the thickness of a genuine flower petal. The pictures on pages 56 and 57 show some of the mouldings that are easily made. Allow to dry out for at least 48 hours before putting on to the cake. Secure the flowers, etc., with a little Royal icing. Always keep the plastic icing in a polythene bag until ready to use, so it does not become too dry. Pictures of moulded flowers are on page 56.

Moulding icing (2)

This icing is a good alternative to that on the left if you have no liquid glucose. It does no enable you to produce such thin petals or flowers as the true plastic icing, but, as it i less brittle, it is excellent to use for making larg(petalled flowers, etc.

1½ level teaspoons powder gelatine	½ oz. (1 teaspoon) white fat (shortening)
1½ tablespoons water or water and lemon juice	12 oz. sieved icing sugar

Put the gelatine and water, or water and lemo(juice, into a basin sufficiently large to mix th(icing. Stand in a saucepan of boiling wate(until the gelatine has dissolved. Stir in the fa(at once, so it melts, then add most of the icin(sugar. Blend thoroughly with a spoon and tur(on to a board. Dust with the remaining suga(and knead thoroughly. Use as plastic icing, an(store in a polythene bag.

Satin icing

Satin icing may be used in place of marzipa(for an 'under-coat', or for the top coat. It is a alternative to fondant, page 34, and plasti(icing, page 53, for it may be rolled out to cov(the cake, or used for moulding. If made a littl(softer than the recipe below it can be use(instead of Royal or butter icings, although it i not suitable for piping. Quantities are similar t(those given in plastic icing, page 53, i.e. allo(2 lb. icing sugar for good coating on 7-inc(cake, with a little left for moulding if wishe(

5 tablespoons lemon juice or water and lemon juice	3 oz. margarine 2 lb. sieved icing sugar

Strain the lemon juice into a pan, add th(margarine, heat gently until melted. Add abo(8 oz. of the icing sugar, stir well until dissolve(Simmer steadily, stirring all the time, *for minutes only.* Remove from the heat, add abo(1 lb. sugar and blend well. Turn into a bowl, (on to a board, and knead in the rest of the suga(to give desired consistency. Roll out and cov(the cake. The more this icing is kneaded th(whiter it becomes, with a satin-like finish. Ti(as wished.

Christmas cake — Australian plastic icing page 53, with yellow church window (run out) and shaping with white icing, also candles, holly, and spray of marzipan lilies with pine kernel hearts. 'Peace and goodwill' lettering in yellow or red or gold tinted Royal Icing.

Christmas cake — the coating is a modified fondant, based on Royal icing. Blend in proportions of 1 lb. sieved icing sugar with 2 oz. warmed glucose, 1 egg white and a little lemon juice. Roll out and use to coat the cake; mould as plastic icing, page 53. The flower centres, and all writing and piping are with Royal icing, made with 8 oz. icing sugar, etc., see page 44. Pipe shell design to complete, and decorate with the moulded flowers etc., and ribbon.

Moulding flowers

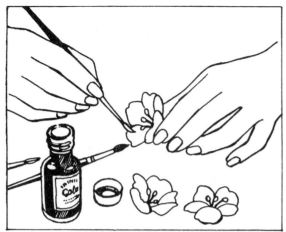

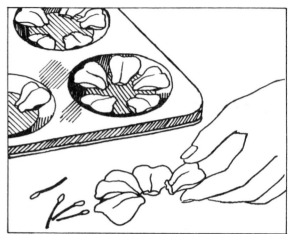

1 Select a suitable icing, either fondant page 34, or marzipan page 38, plastic or satin icings, pages 53 and 54. Check the icing is right consistency, if very hard moisten slightly, if sticky work in more icing sugar. Tint if required, or make the flowers and tint with culinary colourings, put on with a fine brush; this enables more varied shading. To make a simple wild rose make five petals as picture above.

2 Put the petals into a patty tin to support them as they dry, curve each petal in a realistic way. For this particular flower allow the petals to dry. When firm pipe a little Royal icing on to the base of the first petal, then press the second petal on to this. Build up the flower. Pipe tiny 'stamens' in the centre, or insert very fine artificial stamens.

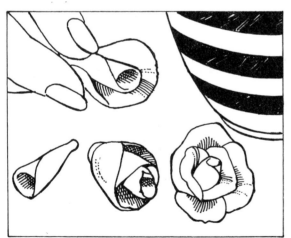

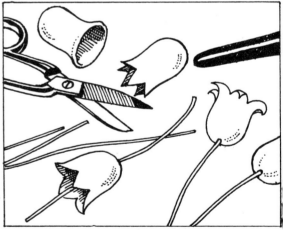

3 To make a rose, start with the centre, form a little icing into a cone. Take a small piece of icing and press out to make the first petal. Either moisten the base of the cone or dip it into a very little Royal icing. Let the first petal curve round the centre, then continue to build up the rose in this way. The picture above shows the various stages of making a rose. Put into a patty tin to dry.

4 To make bell-like flowers, such as hyacinths, take a piece of icing, shape into a bell round the handle of a paint brush. Remove, hold the base carefully with your left hand, snip the petals with small sharp scissors. To assemble a spray either arrange against piped stems, or thread through fine wire. Pull out the petals to form graceful shapes.

More cake decorations

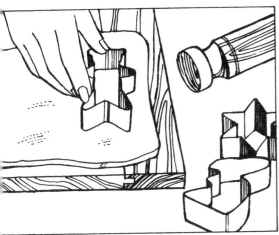

1 Cut outs of animals, etc., are an ideal way of decorating cakes for children. It is possible to buy a variety of cutters (also useful for cutting out biscuits, etc.) but if not available make the shapes in firm cardboard. Roll out the icing, any types mentioned in stage 1 on the opposite page may be used, then cut round the cardboard, or press out the shape with the cutter. Allow to harden.

2 When the shapes are firm they can be tinted or decorated to look more realistic. A duck should have a bright yellow bill and a round dark eye, a small Teddy bear figure has eyes, nose and mouth piped in bright colours. These figures form attractive decorations round the sides of cakes as well as on top of them.

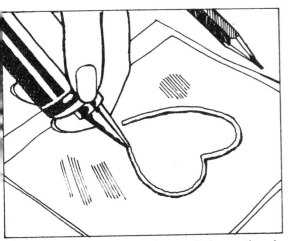

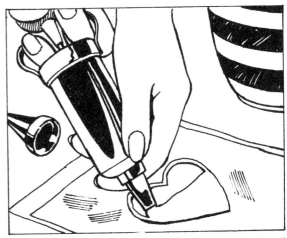

3 Another interesting form of decoration is to make icing plaques. Decide on the figure or shape you wish to make and draw this on a firm piece of card or thick paper. Lay a very thin sheet of waxed paper on top of the drawing. Make either glacé icing, page 12, or Royal icing, page 44. Choose a No. 0 or 1 writing pipe and follow the line of the drawing on the waxed paper, as shown in the picture above.

4 Do not let the outline become too hard and dry, otherwise there will be a mark between outline and filling. To complete the plaque, pipe icing backwards and forwards until the shape is filled. Allow to harden, then add any decorations required. To remove from the paper, take the plaque near the cake to minimise handling. Cut the paper round the figure, then peel it away.

Christening Cakes

The choice of cake depends not only on personal preference, but the average age of the guests. If they are all adult, except the baby to be christened, then you can choose a rich fruit cake as the recipe on page 46, or the moderately rich cake on page 39.

Many young couples though, save the top tier of their wedding cake to be used at the christening. It may be that the icing on this has become very hard with keeping; it can be removed carefully and the cake covered with fresh marzipan and icing.

If there are young children at the christening party it is almost wiser to make a rich plain cake, such as the recipe in the right hand column on this page. This is a sufficiently firm texture to be suitable for both marzipan and Royal icing coatings.

Rich plain cake

10 oz. butter	10 oz. flour (preferably
10 oz. castor sugar	plain with 1½ level
6 large eggs	teaspoons baking
	powder)
	2 oz. ground almonds

Cream the butter and sugar until soft and light. Beat the eggs well, add gradually to the creamed butter. Sieve the flour, or flour and baking powder, with the ground almonds. Fold into the butter mixture very gently. Put into a 9-inch cake tin, lined with greased greaseproof paper. Smooth flat on top, bake in the centre of a slow to very moderate oven, 300–325°F., Gas Mark 2–3, for approximately 2 hours, until firm. Turn out on to a wire cooling tray, but do not remove the paper as this helps to keep the cake moist. Store for several days, before icing, in an airtight tin.

This cake may be flavoured with 1 tablespoon brandy, kirsch or sherry, in which case use 5 large eggs and 1 small egg in the recipe.

To decorate a Christening cake

Choose a white coating, pipe in pink for a girl or blue for a boy. Make sure the icing is a very delicate shade. If preferred, tint the coating icing pink or blue.

Cover the cake with marzipan, for quantities, etc., see pages 38 and 39. Then cover with your selected icing, i.e. Royal, fondant or plastic icings, pages 44, 34 and 53. Decide on the design and pipe around the edge of the cake neatly. When dry, pipe the name of the baby and the date on top, and decorate with a stork and/or small sprays of flowers, see also page 64.

Lining cake tins

Make a double band of greaseproof paper the depth of the tin, plus about 2 inches. Snip along one long side at ½-inch intervals. Line the bottom of the tin with a double round of brown paper (for rich fruit cakes) then put in the side band with the cut edge fitting neatly at the bottom, cover with a double round of greased greaseproof paper. For rich fruit cakes tie a deep band of double brown paper round the outside of tin to protect the cake.

Christening cake – simple and elegant. Coat a fruit cake with marzipan then with Royal icing. Decorate simply in Royal icing using a fine writing pipe, a pipe to make leaves and a rose pipe.

Wedding Cakes

It is quite a responsibility to make and ice a wedding cake at home, but if you give yourself plenty of time this should be a most enjoyable task.

First of all, make sure the cake, if a really rich one, has time to mature. The recipe on the right of this page should be made *at least* 6 weeks before the wedding. The storage time enables it to mature, and if you like a very moist texture soak it with brandy or sherry, as suggested on page 46.

If you decide to ice the cake with Royal icing, then have at least two coats, this ensures a perfect base for piping. Again you must allow time for each coat to harden before putting on the next. I have seen very beautiful wedding cakes covered with the more modern plastic icing and decorated with sprays of flowers to match the bridal bouquet. In this case, just pipe neatly round the bottom edge of the cake. Details of Royal and plastic icings are on pages 44 and 53.

One-tier wedding cake

1 lb. 2 oz. butter	1¼ teaspoons powdered mace
1 lb. 2 oz. moist dark brown sugar	1 lb. 14 oz. currants*
2 teaspoons grated lemon rind	1 lb. 2 oz. seedless or chopped raisins*
9 large eggs	1 lb. 8 oz. sultanas*
3 tablespoons brandy or sweet sherry or rum	12 oz. glacé cherries
1 lb. 2 oz. plain flour	12 oz. mixed candied peel
1¼ teaspoons powdered cinnamon	12 oz. blanched almonds
	4 oz. ground almonds

* if washed, dry for 48 hours at room temperature

(To make a 10-inch square or 11-inch round cake. This cake is very rich, so allow time for it to mature, see previous column, and do prepare the tin carefully, as page 58.) Cream the butter, sugar and lemon rind until soft, do not over-beat, particularly if using an electric mixer.

Beat the eggs and brandy, sherry or rum together, then add gradually to the creamed mixture; if this shows signs of curdling fold in some of the sieved flour. Sieve the flour with the spices, add to the eggs, etc. Mix all the fruit with the halved cherries, chopped peel, chopped almonds and ground almonds, and blend in slowly and steadily. Do mix thoroughly. Put into the prepared tin, smooth flat on top. There are two ways of baking this very rich cake. **A** – and the one I personally prefer – is to allow about 1¼–1½ hours in the centre of a very moderate oven, approximately 325 °F., Gas Mark 3. Watch carefully, the cake should only turn the palest golden colour during this time. Reduce the heat to slow, which for a wedding cake is better, at 275 °F., Gas Mark 1, and cook for a further 3½ hours (approximately), making a total of about 5 hours. **B** – cook in the slow oven for about 6½ hours. Always test in plenty of time – it does not hurt this cake to look at it during cooking. Page 46, at the bottom of rich Christmas cake, gives details of testing. Cool in the tin.

The cooking time for this cake is longer than the Christmas cake, for the tin is fuller as you have more mixture.

If your 10-inch square or 11-inch round tins are not very deep or you want a slightly larger cake, choose an 11-inch square or 12-inch round tin, and bake for 4½–6 hours.

To ice a wedding cake

Choose the type of icing required. Page 38 gives details on marzipan and the quantities required. For a top coat, Royal icing, page 44, is a popular choice. You will need 6 lb. icing sugar, etc., for two coats and a certain amount of piping. If making this in one batch, keep well covered with damp paper or a damp cloth. In view of the fact that each coat must dry well, it probably would be better to make about 2 lb. for the first thin coat, then make up the rest when ready. Read page 44 for information on using a mixer, to avoid over-beating the icing.

As an alternative to Royal icing, consider plastic icing, page 53. You will need 5 lb. icing sugar, etc., for a good coating, and one coat is sufficient. In addition you will need a small amount of Royal icing for piping round the base of the cake, and plastic icing for moulding, see page 54.

Since a wedding cake is cut as part of the ceremony, it is easier, if planning a Royal icing coating (which does become fairly hard) to cut a part of the cake beforehand. This is not necessary with plastic icing, which always remains very easy to cut.

Coat the cake with marzipan as directed on pages 38 to 41, and when quite smooth cut a wedge out of the cake. Put a strip of white satin ribbon, about 1½ inches wide, in a protective band of aluminium foil. Wrap this round the cut-out portion and put back into the cake. Roll the ends of the ribbon firmly, wrap in foil to keep them immaculate, and secure with a pin. This means you can ice the cake quite easily and unroll the ribbon when the cake is complete. The ends may need pressing, but they add to the look of the cake, and all the couple need to do is to insert the knife by one piece of ribbon, press firmly, and the cake is cut.

Stand the cake or cakes on silver cake boards. When buying these remember that a cake becomes about 2 inches bigger when iced and decorated, so choose accordingly.

Decorations for the top of the cake

Mould or pipe flowers; buy or borrow a small vase and fill with real flowers. Stand this in the centre of the top tier.

Three-tier wedding cake

Use twice the amount for the one-tier cake, opposite, i.e. 2 lb. 4 oz. butter, etc.

Prepare the three tins

They can be a 6-inch square or 7-inch round, an 8-inch square or 9-inch round, a 10-inch square or 11-inch round.

This gives a difference of 2 inches between each tier, but the bottom tier can be 3 inches bigger; then use an 11-inch square or 12-inch round tin.

Put *half* the mixture into the largest tin and bake as directed opposite, methods **A** or **B**. Put two-thirds *of the remaining mixture* into the middle sized tin, and bake for a total of about $3\frac{1}{2}$ hours method **A**, or $4\frac{1}{2}$ hours method **B**. The remaining mixture should be baked in the smallest tin for about $2\frac{1}{2}$ hours method **A**, or about $3\frac{1}{4}$ hours method **B**.

To decorate the cake

Decorate each cake as suggested in the left-hand column. The piping or moulding can be exactly the same for each tier, or vary a little. Put each cake on its cake board. To assemble the cakes stand three pillars (you can generally hire these) on the bottom round cake, or four pillars for a square cake. Put the second tier on top. Place the pillars on the second tier, and put the top tier in position. If carrying the cake for a reception do not put together until you reach your destination, carry each tier separately.

Silver wedding cake

This is made like a wedding cake, but all decorations should be silver. You can buy silver bells, horseshoes, etc., for decoration. You may like to pipe the date of the wedding on the cake.

Golden wedding cake

Tint the icing a delicate pale gold, choose gold decorations, and since this is such a very important day, you may like to write a congratulatory message on the cake.

Birthday Cakes

The type of cake chosen for a birthday depends very much upon the age of the person for whom it is intended. In the case of small children, or someone very elderly, it is wise to make a light sponge, such as a Victoria sandwich, page 16, or the whisked sponge, page 26.

If you wish to make the cake well beforehand, then the Victoria sponge is better, since it keeps moist for several days – particularly if filled with butter icing which helps to prevent drying.

For older children and grown-ups, the fruit cake on page 46 is ideal and this can be made some time before the birthday, in fact it improves with being made earlier and given time to mature.

Even if you normally do not pipe on cakes, learn to 'write' with Royal or butter icing, so you can pipe a greeting, as this makes a birthday cake much more personal. See the tips about piping and writing on page 52. If this is your first attempt at 'writing' in icing, then you will find it easier to make capital letters, rather than trying to have a flow of icing. Prick or scratch the greeting on top of the cake so that you position the words easily and evenly.

The most usual greetings would be:

Piping greetings

If piping directly on to the cake worries you then pipe greetings on to a wide band of ribbon. Hold the ribbon taut on a board with drawing pins or icing, and then pipe the greeting (this means you can practise on ribbon until satisfied with the result). When the piping is dry, arrange the ribbon over the top of the cake and secure with a little icing.

Coming-of-age-cake

The cake can be a plain one or a rich fruit, such as pages 46 and 60. It may be decorated as an ordinary birthday cake, it can be ornamented with a key, or be given a more individual touch, as below, or page 65.

Interest cakes

Many people have a hobby, and this can make an excellent theme when decorating a cake, e.g.
Tennis court: make an oblong cake, coat top and sides with pale green icing; when dry, pipe the lines of a tennis court in white icing. Dye a band of curtain net green (or keep it white) and stiffen this. Pipe a band of white along the one edge to look like the top of the net. Secure to the cake with wooden cocktail sticks at each end. Put small toy or moulded figures in position.
Cricket pitch: prepare the cake as above, make 'stumps' in marzipan, arrange small toy or moulded figures in appropriate places.
Football pitch: follow the coating instructions as for tennis court. Make the frame for each goal with fine wire, secure the net to this and pipe around the top of each net. Secure to cake at either end. Make a small ball of marzipan or use a tiny round sweet. Put small toy or moulded 'players' in place.
Circus ring: ice a round cake in a pretty colour. Put a band of stiffened net round the edge to denote the 'ring'. Arrange figures and animals on top of the cake.
Skating rink: coat the cake in white with a band around as above, put 'skaters' in place.
Ballet scene: build up 'scenery' as on a stage on a round or square cake, then arrange the dancers in front of this.

A birthday cake – with a new look. Coat with chocolate butter icing (see pages 13–15). Decorate with chocolate figures. You can buy these all ready to use.

Novelty cakes

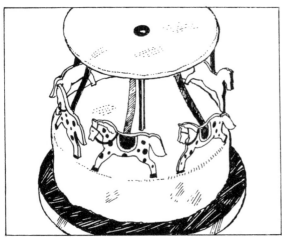

1 *Merry-go-round:* cut a round of card, slightly smaller than the round cake. Coat in gay coloured icing to match the cake. Stand a centre 'pole' – a barley stick or bright knitting needle will do – in the middle of the cake, support the 'roof' in position. Arrange toy or moulded animals around the top of the cake, attach ribbon streamers from these to the roof of the Merry-go-round.

2 *Maypole cake:* make a central 'pole' as cake No. 1. Put tiny toy figures around the cake and attach streamers from each figure to the top of the 'pole'. The cake can be covered with any coloured icing, but the most appropriate would be pale green to look like grass. If wished, pipe stars round edge or sprays of flowers around the sides. Candles and greetings could be on the cake board.

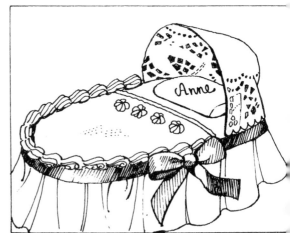

3 *Humpty-Dumpty cake:* stand a square or long-shaped cake on end to look like a 'wall'. Coat with icing and when dry secure to a cake board. Pipe lines to make the shape of 'bricks'. Form 'Humpty' in marzipan, or mould in icing, or even hard boil an egg. Make legs of icing, pipe a face on part of the oval shape. Either perch on the 'wall', or allow him to fall on to the cake board. Arrange toy soldiers around.

4 *Cot cake:* make a cake in an oval pie-dish (this cooks in a little shorter time than in a round tin). Coat the top and sides in white icing. When dry, pipe tiny flowers over part of the top for a cover, with a 'pillow' of moulded icing. Pipe flowers or the baby's name on this. Drape the sides of the cot with real muslin, or thin moulded icing, as page 54. This makes a christening or birthday cake.

More novelty cakes

5 *Book cake:* shape an oblong cake to look like an opened book, see sketch above. or a very large 'book' use two square cakes nd a narrow strip of cake through the middle to give correct proportions. Coat the cake with hosen type of icing and when dry pipe greetings n top. Put a book-mark of ribbon, or ribbon and owers, down the centre. Suitable for most ccasions.

6 *Parcel cake:* make a square or oblong cake into a parcel. Coat with light brown or gay coloured icing; when dry, pipe the lines of string. Put 'blobs' of red sealing wax here and there, and make stamps either in moulded icing, by piping, or use real stamps. Address the parcel to the person in whose honour the cake is being made. Put candles and greetings round the side.

7 *Fort cake:* bake a square cake, coat with marzipan, make small squares or oblongs, lace on top of the cake. Cover with white or ther icing. When dry, pipe 'windows' and loors'. Make a 'drawbridge' of marzipan, oated with dark icing, attach to the cake with wists of icing or marzipan. Put soldiers on top f and around the fort, decorate with flags, put uns in position.

8 *Casket cake:* bake a round or square cake. Cut a slice from the top, cut this into two sections for the lid. Coat the cake and top pieces with icing. This can be marzipan, butter icing, plastic icing, etc. A woven design looks very good. Replace one half of the top. Lay moulded or real flowers, sweets, liqueur choco-lates, or tiny crackers, on top of the cake. Place the other half of the lid lightly in position.

Gâteaux and Pastries

The following pages give a selection of cakes, all decorated to make them look interesting and suitable for special occasions. Some are based on well-known Continental gâteaux. The type of decoration and icing suggested for each cake gives the best result, but if you wish to change it then choose one that has the same kind of texture, i.e. replace cream with a mock cream or soft butter icing.

Gâteau mille feuilles

for the pastry	filling and decoration
8 oz. plain flour	4 tablespoons apricot jam
pinch salt	or glaze, page 67
good squeeze lemon juice	½ pint thick cream, or mock
water to mix	cream (right)
8 oz. butter or luxury	glacé icing made with 8 oz.
margarine	icing sugar, page 10
	2 oz. blanched almonds

Sieve the flour and salt into a basin, add the lemon juice and enough water to make an elastic dough. Roll out to an oblong shape. Make sure the butter or margarine is not too hard; luxury margarine softens quickly, but bring butter out of the refrigerator some time beforehand. Place the fat in the centre of the dough, fold this like an envelope. Turn the dough, at right angles, then 'rib' it (this means depress at intervals with the rolling pin), roll out lightly to an oblong once more. Fold again in the shape of an envelope. Put in a cool place for about 15 minutes. Bring out, roll again. Continue like this until the pastry has had 7 rollings and 7 foldings. Chill well in between. Roll out the pastry until wafer-thin, cut into 3 rounds or squares. Place these on slightly damped baking trays or sheets, bake towards the top of a hot to very hot oven, 450–475°F., Gas Mark 7–8, for about 6 minutes, then lower the heat to very moderate for a further 5–6 minutes, or until the pastry is firm, well risen and golden-coloured.

To decorate the gâteau

Allow the pastry to become cold. If using apricot glaze, prepare and allow it to cool. Whip the cream, or make the mock or vanilla cream, see below. Real cream may be sweetened if wished. Trim the edges of each of the rounds, or squares, with a very sharp knife; make sure each piece of pastry is exactly the same size as the others. Spread the first piece of pastry with half the jam or glaze, then half the cream or mock cream. Put the second piece of pastry on top, cover with jam or glaze, and the cream. Make the glacé icing as page 10, and coat the top piece of pastry with this. If wished, it can be made into a feathered pattern, as page 32. Lift this carefully over the rest of the gâteau. Split the almonds and brown for a few minutes in the oven or under the grill. Cool, sprinkle on top of the half set icing. Serve when fresh.

Mock cream

1 level tablespoon corn-	few drops vanilla essence
flour or custard powder	1 oz. castor sugar
¼ pint milk	2 oz. unsalted butter

Blend the cornflour, or custard powder, with the cold milk. Put into a pan with the essence and sugar, stir over a low heat until a smooth thick mixture. Spoon into a basin, cover with damp greaseproof paper to prevent a skin forming, and allow to cool. Cream the butter in another basin until soft, then gradually beat in teaspoons of the cold cornflour mixture; continue adding until a smooth thick mixture. Keeps 2–3 days.

Vanilla cream (Confectioner's custard)

1 tablespoon cornflour	2 egg yolks
¼ pint milk	4 tablespoons milk
1–2 oz. castor sugar	4 tablespoons thick cream
few drops vanilla essence	

Blend the cornflour and ¼ pint milk, put into a pan with the sugar and vanilla, cook until thickened. Blend the egg yolks with rest of the milk. Add to the cornflour mixture. Cook *without boiling* until thick. Cool as previous recipe, fold in whipped cream. Keeps 1–2 days.

Choux pastry

2 oz. butter or margarine
¼ pint water
pinch salt

few drops vanilla essence
3 oz. flour, preferably plain
2–3 eggs, see method

Put the butter or margarine, water, pinch salt and essence into a pan. Heat until the butter or margarine has melted. Remove from the heat and stir in the flour, then return to the heat and cook gently, stirring well, until the mixture forms a soft smooth ball and leaves the sides of the pan. Once again remove from the heat and cool slightly. Add the beaten egg, a little at a time, and continue until 2 eggs have been incorporated. Unless the eggs are very large you will probably need a little yolk from the third egg, for the mixture should be sufficiently firm to hold a shape, but soft enough to pipe or spread. Use as below.

Cream buns and éclairs

ingredients as choux
pastry (above)

¼–½ pint thick cream
little icing sugar

Make the choux pastry and put the mixture into a piping bag with a ½–1-inch plain pipe. Pipe small 'blobs' on to a lightly greased baking tray, leaving room to spread out. The mixture makes about 8 really large buns, 12 medium sized, or about 16 little buns. Bake for approximately 20–35 minutes (depending upon the size). Start with a moderate to moderately hot oven, 375–400°F., Gas Mark 5–6, and lower this to very moderate after about 15 minutes. Beware of draughts if you are looking into the oven. The cakes are cooked when pale golden and firm. Cool away from a draught, then split, remove any slightly uncooked mixture if necessary and 'dry out' for a few minutes in the oven. When cold, fill with the cream, or you could use mock cream or vanilla cream (left). Dust with sieved icing sugar, or coat with icing as éclairs below. Either eat when fresh, or freeze, complete with filling, then defrost at room temperature and serve at once.

Éclairs are prepared in the same way as cream buns, but are piped with a ¼–½-inch pipe, or spooned into fingers. Bake for about 20–25 minutes, fill and decorate, see right.

To decorate éclairs

While one may dust a cream bun just with icing sugar, it is usual to ice éclairs, having filled them with cream or an alternative, as given in cream buns (left).

Choose either a glacé icing, pages 10–12, or make an icing with melted chocolate, as below. The amount given below is enough to coat about 16 éclairs, which can be made with the basic recipe given on the left. Eat when fresh, or freeze, complete with icing, as cream buns.

Melted chocolate icing

3 oz. chocolate*
2 tablespoons water

4 oz. sieved icing sugar
few drops vanilla essence

* choose bitter, plain or couverture

You will find chocolate sold specially for icing, and this is really the best type to choose, for it melts well and gives a good flavour. Break the chocolate into pieces, put into a basin or the top of a double saucepan. Add the water and stand over a pan of hot, but not boiling, water. Heat gently until the chocolate has melted, then remove from the heat and stir well. Add the icing sugar and the vanilla essence, beat together. Cool sufficiently to become a fairly soft spreading consistency, and coat the top of the éclairs with this.

Paris Brest

ingredients as choux
pastry (left)

filling
vanilla cream, page 66

topping
caramel icing, page 70,
or 4–5 tablespoons jam
glaze (below)
1–2 oz. blanched almonds

Make the choux pastry, and pipe in rings with a ¼–½-inch pipe. Bake as cream buns, on the left, but allow only about 20 minutes. Cool, split, and fill with the cold vanilla cream. Coat the top with the caramel, or glaze, and with flaked almonds. Eat when fresh, or freeze as cream buns.

Jam glaze: boil jam with a very little water until dissolved, sieve and use.

Coffee fudge cake

5 oz. butter or margarine
5 oz. castor sugar
3 small eggs
1 tablespoon coffee essence
5 oz. flour (with plain
    flour use 1½ teaspoons
    baking powder)

1 oz. cornflour

filling and topping
fudge icing, below
little apricot jam

Cream the butter or margarine and sugar until soft and light. Beat the eggs and coffee essence, and add gradually to the creamed mixture. Sieve the flour, or flour and baking powder, and cornflour, then fold into the rest of the ingredients. Grease and flour two 7–8-inch sandwich tins, or line the bottoms with greased greaseproof paper. Divide the mixture between these, and bake for approximately 25 minutes just above the centre of a moderate oven, 350–375°F., Gas Mark 4–5, until firm to the touch. Turn out and allow to cool.

The cornflour in this recipe gives a firm, fine texture, that blends well with the fudge icing, but if preferred use the coffee cake, on page 17, which is based on the true Victoria sandwich, and fill that with fudge icing.

Make the fudge icing, as below. Spread one cake with a little jam, then half the icing. Put the second cake on top, spread with a layer of jam, then the fudge icing. The jam prevents the rather firm icing spoiling the texture of the cake. Fudge icing is so attractive to look at that it needs no decoration, but if you wish to add chopped nuts to the filling, then decorate with nuts on top. Eat within 2–3 days.

Fudge icing

12 oz. granulated sugar
4 tablespoons water
1½ oz. butter or luxury
    margarine

vanilla essence
small can full cream
    sweetened condensed
    milk

Put the sugar and water into a *strong* saucepan, stir until the sugar has dissolved then add the butter or margarine, up to ½ teaspoon vanilla essence and the condensed milk. Boil steadily, stirring most of the time, until the mixture reaches 238°F., or forms a soft ball when tested in cold water, see page 36 for details of this. Beat until cloudy, then use at once.

Variations on fudge icing

If wished, use brown sugar in place of granulated; the only drawback of this is that it makes a very dark fudge icing, which does not look as attractive on a cake — but it tastes delicious. It is, therefore, quite a good idea to choose this for a filling and leave the top of the cake uniced, or use a different type of icing for the top.

½ pint thin cream may be used in place of condensed milk in the icing (opposite), in which case use only 2 tablespoons water.

Flavourings for fudge icing

Use rum, almond or other essences.

Add finely grated lemon or orange rind, but do not use fruit juice, otherwise the mixture will curdle.

To give a chocolate flavour add a tablespoon cocoa, or 2 tablespoons chocolate powder, when the mixture has reached 238°F. Beat well to make sure the chocolate fudge icing will be quite smooth.

Orange fudge gâteau

ingredients as orange
    sponge, page 18

filling and coating
5 oz. butter
10 oz. sieved icing sugar
2 teaspoons finely grated
    orange rind
2 oz. blanched almonds

topping
fudge icing made with
    6 oz. granulated sugar
    2 tablespoons water
    nearly 1 oz. butter or
    luxury margarine
    ½–1 teaspoon finely grated
    orange rind
    ½ small can sweetened
    condensed milk

Make and bake the orange cake as the recipe on page 18, and allow this to cool. Well cream the butter, icing sugar and orange rind, until soft and light. Do not make the fudge icing too early. It is put on the cake last. Use part of the butter icing to sandwich the two cakes together. Spread most of the remainder around the sides. Chop or flake the almonds, brown in the oven or under the grill, if wished, but they can be used without browning. Roll the cake in these, see page 6. Make the fudge icing and when cloudy spread over the top of the cake; pipe with remainder of the orange butter icing. Eat when fresh.

Chocolate rum gâteau

4 oz. chocolate*
6 oz. butter
6 oz. castor sugar
4 large eggs
4 oz. flour, preferably
   plain
4 oz. ground almonds

filling and topping
4 oz. chocolate*
3 oz. butter
6 oz. sieved icing sugar
1–2 tablespoons rum

decoration
4 oz. chocolate*
little sieved icing sugar

*choose bitter, plain, couverture or cooking chocolate

Melt the chocolate for the cake. To do this, break it into pieces and put it into the top of a double saucepan, or basin, over hot water; do not allow the water to boil. Leave the chocolate until melted, do not stir at this stage. Put on one side to cool slightly. Cream the butter and sugar until soft and light. Separate the eggs, and beat the yolks into the butter mixture, then add the melted chocolate; do not waste any, for this is important to give the correct consistency to the cake. Sieve or mix the flour and ground almonds and fold gently into the rest of the ingredients. Finally add the stiffly beaten egg whites, gently and carefully. Line an 8–9-inch cake tin with greased and floured greaseproof paper. Spoon in the mixture. Bake in the centre of a slow to very moderate oven, 300–325°F., Gas Mark 2–3, for approximately 45–50 minutes, until just firm to the touch. Do not overcook this cake, for it should be pleasantly moist. Allow to cool.

Melt the 8 oz. chocolate for the filling and decoration, pour half on to a slab or flat tin to make chocolate curls (chocolate caraque), see page 43, stage 3. Add the rest of the melted chocolate to the creamed butter and sugar. Beat the rum gradually into this; take care the mixture does not curdle. Split the cake through the centre and cover the base with half the chocolate rum mixture. Put on the other half of the cake and top with rest of the chocolate rum icing. Leave this to become fairly firm. Make the chocolate caraque, and when firm arrange on the cake top. To give a striped effect to the decoration, lay two bands of greaseproof paper gently over the chocolate curls. Shake icing sugar through a fine sieve, remove the paper. This cake keeps for up to two weeks.

Austrian Sachertorte

5 oz. chocolate*
1 tablespoon water
5 oz. butter
6 oz. sieved icing sugar
5 eggs
5 oz. flour (with plain
   flour use 1¼ teaspoons
   baking powder)
1 oz. cornflour

topping
3–4 tablespoons apricot
   jam
1 tablespoon water, rum or
   brandy
4–5 oz. chocolate*
½ oz. butter

* see left

Melt the chocolate as the recipe on the left, but in this case add the water to give a softer mixture; cool slightly. Cream the butter and sugar until soft and light, add the eggs very gradually, beating well, then slowly beat in the melted chocolate. If the mixture shows signs of curdling, fold in a little sieved flour. Sieve the flour, or flour and baking powder, and cornflour, fold carefully into the chocolate mixture. Line a 9–10-inch cake tin with greased and floured greaseproof paper. Put in the mixture and bake for approximately 45 minutes in the centre of a very moderate oven, 325–350°F., Gas Mark 3–4. Test by pressing gently. Turn out carefully, allow to cool. Cover the top of the cake with warmed apricot jam. Cool this, and then coat with melted chocolate icing, made by heating the water, rum or brandy, and chocolate with the small piece of butter. For directions on melting chocolate see the cake recipe on the left, or pictured in stage 1, page 43. This keeps a week.

Mocha rum gâteau

ingredients as Victoria
   sandwich, page 16

to moisten
¼ pint strong coffee
2–3 tablespoons rum

filling and topping
4 oz. butter
6 oz. sieved icing sugar
2 oz. ground almonds
1 tablespoon cocoa
little sieved icing sugar

Make and bake the cake in one tin (preferably loose-based) as page 16. Cool, split into three layers. Put one layer back into the tin. Mix coffee and rum, moisten the sponge with 3 tablespoonfuls. Cover with a third of the filling, made by blending butter, sugar, almonds and cocoa. Repeat with the rest of the sponge, etc., but hold back one-third of the filling. Leave 24 hours; turn out. Top with the filling and icing sugar. This keeps several days, and it also freezes well.

Using caramel icing

Caramel cream gâteau

Genoese pastry
3 oz. butter
3 large eggs
4 oz. castor sugar
3 oz. flour, preferably plain

topping
caramel icing (below and
   right)
¼ pint thick cream

filling
¼ pint thick cream

Melt the butter carefully, allow to cool. Beat the eggs and sugar until sufficiently thick to see the mark of the whisk. Sieve the flour at least once, and fold this into the eggs and sugar. Next, fold in the melted butter gently but thoroughly.

Grease and flour two 7–8-inch sandwich tins, or line the base with greased and floured paper. Divide the Genoese pastry between the two tins, and bake above the centre of a moderate oven, 350–375°F., Gas Mark 4–5, for approximately 16–18 minutes, until firm to the touch. Turn out carefully and cool. Spread the bottom cake with the firmly whipped cream, this could be sweetened slightly, if wished. Make the caramel icing as instructions on the right, and ingredients given below, and spoon this very carefully over the top cake. Allow to set, then mark into segments with a sharp knife, see stage 2. Lift this on to the bottom cake, and whip the rest of the cream. Pipe a wide border of cream around the edge of the caramel icing. This cake should be eaten when fresh, for the icing tends to become sticky with exposure to the air.

Note. Genoese pastry, as given in the recipe above, is an excellent basis for many cakes. It keeps moist longer than the sponge cake on page 26, but is lighter than a Victoria sandwich, page 16.

Caramel icing

6 oz. loaf or granulated
   sugar
6 tablespoons water

Put the sugar and water into a strong saucepan and stir until the sugar has dissolved. This is very important, for if the sugar is not stirred at the beginning it can crystallise, and will not turn to golden brown caramel. When the sugar has dissolved, boil without stirring until golden brown, see right.

1 Make the caramel icing as the recipe, left do not allow it to become too brown, for it continues cooking in the pan. Leave in the pan until slightly sticky in texture, then pour or spread over the top of the cake or one layer of the cake, as the picture above. Do this slowly, so the caramel does not 'drip' down the sides of the cake.

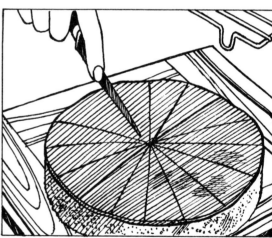

2 Leave the caramel to set on the cake. When quite firm, mark into sections with a sharp knife. It is advisable to do this on one layer only, as in the recipe on the left, for if you try to do this when the cake is sandwiched with a soft filling, such as cream, you will make this 'ooze out' in a very unattractive manner. This caramel can be added to butter icings if wished.

Crumb gâteau

oz. crisp breadcrumbs
large eggs
oz. castor sugar

icing and decoration
6 oz. icing sugar
1 tablespoon Maraschino
Maraschino cherries
small piece angelica

filling
vanilla cream, page 66

If making your own crumbs make sure they are very fine, and crisp them slowly in the oven until very pale golden brown. The packet crisp crumbs can be used, but they make a rather dark cake. Whisk the eggs and sugar until really thick, then fold in the crumbs. There is no flour in this cake. Put into two 7—8-inch sandwich tins, lined with greased and floured paper. Bake for approximately 15 minutes above the centre of a moderate oven, 350—375°F., Gas Mark 4—5, until firm to the touch. Turn out, remove paper from the cakes while warm. Do this carefully, for they are very fragile. If the paper seems to be sticking to the cakes, brush it with a pastry brush dipped in cold water. Allow the cakes to cool. Make the vanilla cream, as page 66, and use to sandwich the cakes together. Make the icing by blending the sugar and Maraschino together, see page 12 for information on glacé icing. Spread over the top of the cake, and when nearly set decorate with well drained Maraschino cherries and leaves of angelica.

Crumb cream gâteau

Make the cake as above. When cooked, sandwich together with whipped cream, sweetened lightly and flavoured with brandy or curaçao.

Spread more cream over the top, and decorate with coarsely grated chocolate.

Austrian hazelnut gâteau

This is made as the crumb gâteau, but instead of crumbs use ground hazelnuts. These can be purchased ready-ground, or put the nuts into an electric blender or through a mincer. Do not try and remove the skins; they add flavour to the cake.

This cake is delicious sandwiched together with sliced fresh or canned peaches and cream, and topped with whipped cream and peaches. All the cakes above should be eaten fresh.

American shortcake

4 oz. butter or fat
(shortening)
4 oz. castor sugar
2 small eggs
8 oz. flour (with plain
flour use 2 teaspoons
baking powder)

filling and topping
½ pint thick cream or
mock cream, as page 66
1 lb. fresh fruit
sugar to taste

Cream the butter or fat and sugar until soft and light. Gradually beat in the eggs, then add the flour. The cake should be a soft rolling consistency. Divide the mixture in two, and press each half into a 7—8-inch sandwich tin, which should be well greased and floured. Each piece of cake dough can be rolled out to fit the tin, if wished, or simply place the dough in the tin and press with the tips of your fingers until it fits neatly. Bake above the centre of a moderately hot oven, 400°F., Gas Mark 5—6, for about 20 minutes, until firm to the touch. Cool in the tins for a few minutes, as the shortcake is inclined to be fragile while warm. Turn out and cool. Whip the cream, use just under half to cover one of the cakes. Top with half the whole or sliced fruit — use fresh raspberries, strawberries, peaches, etc., and dust with sugar. Put the second cake on top, and spread with some of the cream. Decorate with whole fruit, or neatly sliced fruit, and pipe with the remaining cream.

Note. Always be careful when whipping cream, especially for piping, that it is not over-whipped, for it then curdles and is impossible to re-whip without it separating. Shortcakes should be eaten when fresh, although they can be prepared as above and frozen. Thaw out at room temperature; serve at once.

Fruit sponge gâteau

Both the Victoria sandwich and the whisked sponge, pages 16 and 26, can be used in the same way as the shortcake, above. As the Victoria sandwich is a little more 'solid' than the sponge, it is a good idea to let the gâteau stand for a few hours in a cool place, so the fruit and cream filling can moisten the cake. The chocolate, coffee and fruit-flavoured sponges could be used.

All gâteaux using fresh cream must be eaten when fresh, or should be frozen for safe storage.

Valentine Gâteaux

Many of the cakes given in this book are ideal as the basis for a Valentine or engagement party gâteau. It is traditional to make this in the form of a heart, and baking tins of this shape are obtainable quite easily.

The cooking time for a Valentine cake will be very similar to that of a sandwich cake, if you are using a shallow heart-shaped tin.

Keep the decorations for Valentine cakes pretty and delicate looking, as one would expect for a rather 'romantic' theme. The recipes and sketches on these pages give a variety of suggestions.

Praline Valentine

Genoese pastry	filling and topping
3 oz. butter	praline, see below
3 large eggs	6 oz. butter
4 oz. castor sugar	10 oz. sieved icing sugar
3 oz. flour, preferably plain	few drops almond essence

Make the Genoese pastry as the recipe on page 70, and put the mixture into a large shallow heart-shaped tin, which should be well greased and floured. Bake above the centre of a moderate oven, 350–375°F., Gas Mark 4–5, for about 16–18 minutes, until firm to the touch. Turn out and allow to cool. Make the praline as the recipe below. (Since this takes time to prepare and cool, it is advisable to prepare either while the cake is cooking or beforehand.) Cream the butter and sugar together, and add the almond essence to taste. Coat the top and sides of the heart-shaped cake with the icing, smooth and flat as possible. Crush the praline and press it against the sides and top of the cake. Decorate with a bow of ribbon. If wished, pipe a border of butter icing around base and top edge of the cake. If you do this, then make up more icing, i.e. use an extra 2 oz. butter and 3–4 oz. sugar. This cake keeps several days, although the praline tends to become sticky if exposed to the air, so keep in an airtight tin.

Praline

3 oz. blanched almonds	4 oz. granulated or loaf
3 tablespoons water	sugar

Chop the almonds fairly finely. Put the water and sugar into a strong saucepan. Stir until the sugar has dissolved, then allow the mixture to boil steadily, without stirring, until it begins to turn the faintest golden colour. Add the almonds, stir once to make sure they are well mixed with the syrup then continue boiling until the sweetmeat turns a real golden brown. Pour from the pan on to a marble slab or tin, and allow to cool and set. Crush with a rolling pin and use as a decoration, as in the recipe above, or add to cream or butter icing in fillings.

The praline will keep crisp if put on to a fairly firm butter icing, as the recipe above, providing it is stored in a tin.

Decorating Valentine cakes

1 Coat the cake with white or pale pink glacé icing, see pages 10–12. When nearly dry, press small heart-shapes, made from tinted marzipan, against the sides of the cake. See pages 38–41 for details of making marzipan, etc. Pipe tiny rosettes or stars in butter icing around each heart-shape. Details of butter icing are on page 13. Put a spray of moulded or fresh flowers on top of the cake.

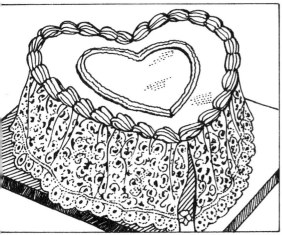

2 Coat the cake with glacé, fondant, or plastic icing, see pages 10–12, 34 and 53. Pipe a narrow line of butter icing, page 13, around the top edge and base of the cake. Press fine lace into the top edging, so the cake looks like an old-fashioned Valentine. Decorate with piping in butter icing.

Marzipan Valentine gâteau

5 oz. butter or margarine	3 oz. castor sugar
5 oz. castor sugar	3 oz. sieved icing sugar
3 large eggs	few drops almond essence
few drops almond essence	1 small egg
5 oz. flour (preferably	
plain with ½ teaspoon	**decoration**
baking powder)	3 oz. butter
2 oz. ground almonds	6 oz. sieved icing sugar
4 oz. glacé cherries	few drops almond essence
	few drops cochineal
topping	glacé cherries
3 tablespoons jam	
6 oz. ground almonds	

Cream the butter or margarine and sugar until soft and light. Gradually beat in the eggs and almond essence, then fold in the sieved flour, or flour and baking powder, together with the ground almonds. Halve the cherries, if very sticky flour lightly before folding them into the mixture. Line the base of a heart-shaped tin, about 10 inches from top to the point, with greased and floured paper. Bake the cake in the centre of a slow to very moderate oven, 300–325°F., Gas Mark 2–3, for about 1¼ hours, until firm to the touch. Turn out carefully and allow to cool. It is a good idea to leave the cake for 24 hours before coating with marzipan, etc. Brush the sides and top of the cake with warmed sieved jam. Make the marzipan with the ground almonds, castor and icing sugar, almond essence and enough egg to make a rolling consistency. Roll out thinly, see page 38, and put over the cake, press gently until this forms a perfect heart-shape, see the picture of coating cakes on page 40. Trim the base of the cake neatly. Cream the butter, icing sugar and almond essence together, tint pale pink.

Put into a piping bag or syringe with a small star pipe. Lift the cake on to a round or heart-shaped cake board. Pipe a neat border around the top edge of the cake and around the base. Decorate with halved glacé cherries.

Meringue Valentine

Make the meringue mixture as page 75, using 3 egg whites, etc. Cut out two heart-shaped pieces of greaseproof paper. Oil lightly and cover with the meringue mixture. Bake as the Pavlova on page 75. Sandwich with cream, or cream and fruit, and decorate as Pavlova; do this just before serving.

Biscuits

Several of the biscuit recipes in this section have a double purpose; they can be served separately for tea, or they can be used to decorate a cake. Most biscuits, particularly those with a high percentage of golden syrup, become soft when exposed to the air for more than an hour or so. They should, therefore, be iced or filled with cream (as a brandy snap), or put on the cake at the last minute.

Marshmallow shortbreads

3 oz. butter	**marshmallow frosting**
3 oz. castor sugar	2 oz. marshmallows
3 oz. plain flour	2 teaspoons milk
1 oz. rice flour or cornflour	1 egg white
	2 teaspoons castor sugar
little extra rice flour or cornflour	
	2 tablespoons jam

Cream the butter with half the sugar, then work in the sieved flour and rice flour, or cornflour. Mix thoroughly, add the rest of the sugar. Dust a pastry board with rice flour or cornflour, roll out the dough to $\frac{1}{4}$ inch in thickness. Cut into small shapes. Put on to ungreased baking trays, prick lightly with a fork and bake in the centre of a very moderate to moderate oven, 325–350°F., Gas Mark 3–4, for approximately 15 minutes. Cool on trays, store in an airtight tin until ready to serve, or to ice; this should be done an hour or so before serving.

To make the marshmallow frosting: put the marshmallows and milk into a basin. Stand over a pan of hot water until marshmallows have *just* melted. Allow to cool, but not become firm again. Whisk egg white until stiff, gradually whisk in the sugar, then fold the meringue mixture into marshmallows. Stand for about 7–10 minutes to become quite firm in texture. Spread the biscuits with the jam, then top with marshmallow frosting. Eat the iced biscuits when fresh. Shortbread keeps for weeks and the icing for 2–3 days. Makes about 16–20 biscuits.

Brandy snaps

4 oz. butter, margarine or fat (shortening)	1–2 teaspoons ground ginger
4 oz. castor sugar	squeeze lemon juice, optional
4 level tablespoons golden syrup	
4 oz. flour, *less* 2 level teaspoons	

Put the butter or other fat into a large saucepan with the sugar and golden syrup. Heat gently until the fat has melted, then remove from the heat and stir in the flour, sieved with the ginger. Add just a squeeze of lemon juice, if wished. Grease several baking trays, do not flour them. Put teaspoons of the mixture on each tray, allowing plenty of room for the mixture to spread out to become about 3–4 inches in width. As you need to handle the biscuits while warm, it is a good idea to put only one tray in the oven at a time. Bake for about 8–10 minutes, in a very moderate to moderately hot oven, 325–350°F., Gas Mark 3–4, in or as near the centre as possible. They should be golden coloured, but check after 5–6 minutes. Bring out the first tray, put in the next to cook. Leave the biscuits for about 2 minutes, then test to see if cooked. You should be able to slip a palette knife under them quite easily. To roll the brandy snaps, put round the handle of a lightly greased wooden spoon, hold in position for a few seconds to set, lift off. If you wish to make cones, which look more attractive on a cake, wrap round the outside of lightly greased cream horn tins. If the biscuits on the baking tray become a little set and difficult to remove, warm for 1–2 minutes then continue as above. When set and cold, store in a *very airtight* tin. If doubtful about the tin being airtight, seal with sticking tape. Serve plain, or fill with piped whipped cream just before serving. Eat when fresh if filled with cream. Plain brandy snaps keep for weeks in a tin. Makes about 30.

Brandy snap gâteau

Make a Victoria sandwich, page 16. Fill with whipped cream, flavoured with ground ginger and sweetened, or add chopped preserved or crystallised ginger. Spread top with cream, decorate with brandy snaps filled with cream.

Prepare cake earlier, top with brandy snaps at the last minute.

Meringues

2 egg whites	4 oz. castor sugar or 2 oz. castor and 2 oz. sieved icing sugar

It is important when making meringues to see that the bowl in which you intend to whisk the egg whites is very free from grease, as even a small particle could prevent the whites becoming as stiff as possible. If you keep the eggs in a refrigerator, remove for a few hours if possible so they are not too cold. On the other hand, too hot a room slows up whisking, in which case cool them very slightly before whisking. Whisk the egg whites by hand, or mixer, until they stand in peaks, do not over-whisk, for this makes a very dry and crumbly meringue. If using two kinds of sugar, mix well together. I find little advantage in using icing sugar, it tends to give a drier meringue. Whisk in up to half the sugar very gradually, if using a mixer lower the speed as you do this, then fold in the rest of the sugar. If you whisk in all the sugar you tend to have a rather dry meringue. Oil the baking tray or trays very lightly with olive oil or a very little butter. Take a spoonful of the mixture, put it on to the tray, then shape neatly on top with a second spoon. If preferred put the mixture into a piping bag with a $\frac{1}{4}$—$\frac{1}{2}$-inch plain or rose pipe, and pipe rounds or finger-shapes.

Bake in the coolest part of a very slow oven, 250–275°F., Gas Mark $\frac{1}{2}$–1, for $1\frac{1}{2}$–2 hours. If you can set the oven even lower, then do so and allow $2\frac{1}{2}$–3 hours. Both times are for round meringues, finger-shapes cook more quickly; they are ready when firm to touch, but still white. Remove the meringues from the tray while warm using a palette knife. If they show signs of 'sticking', warm the knife in hot water, then dry and insert under the biscuits. Cool, and store in an airtight tin. They keep for months.

2 egg whites give about 6 very large shells, or 10–12 medium round shells, but up to 24 finger-shapes. These are very useful as a border round a gâteau, or to serve with ice cream.

To tint meringues add a few drops of colouring to the egg whites before adding the sugar. Keep colours pale. It is advisable to beat the egg whites again when you have added the colouring.

Meringues Chantilly

Whip thick cream, flavour with a little vanilla essence, and sweeten. Sandwich the meringues with this mixture, and place in paper cases or on a dish. If wished, pipe a band of the whipped cream over the top of each pair of meringues, and decorate with a glacé or Maraschino cherry, and leaves of angelica. When the meringue cases are filled they should be served within an hour or so, otherwise they become very soft. They can, however, be frozen — the cream becomes hard, but the meringues remain as normal, due to the high sugar content. Thaw out for the cream to soften, and serve at once.

Pavlova

4–5 egg whites	1 teaspoon cornflour
8–10 oz. sugar, see left	1 teaspoon malt vinegar

A Pavlova is a meringue-shape, that can be varied in many ways, see below. The minimum number of egg whites to give a good sized Pavlova is 4, but 5 egg whites enable you to have two very good layers, or a deep band around one layer. The cornflour and vinegar may be omitted, but they help to give a firm crisp outside and a slightly 'sticky' inside. The shape may be stored for some weeks and filled when required. If serving freshly cooked and cooled, you can shorten the cooking time slightly if you like an under-cooked meringue. This type does not keep well.

Whisk the egg whites as the recipe left, then add the sugar, blended with the cornflour. Fold in the vinegar. Make the mixture into three thin, or two thicker, layers, or form or pipe into a flan-shape with a deep band around the side. This can be formed with a knife or a more professional result is obtained by piping. Put the mixture on oiled tins, or make shapes from greaseproof paper and oil or butter these.

Bake as meringues, allowing 3–4 hours; remove from the tins. Cool, store. Fill the Pavlova, or sandwich the layers together with whipped cream or Crème Chantilly (above). Top with fresh or well drained fruit. When the case is filled it should be used within an hour or so. It can, however, be frozen, see Meringues Chantilly, above.

Petits~fours

This term denotes small cakes, biscuits, etc. These can be served after a meal with coffee, or at tea-time, and make excellent presents if packed in an attractive manner.

It is possible to buy small sweetmeat paper cases, and the petits-fours should be put in these if possible.

There are a number of recipes suitable for petits-fours in this book, for example:

a) sponge fancies, page 33. Make these about 1 inch in size, decorate with delicate piping, tiny pieces of cherry, nut, angelica or crystallised petals, as right.

b) marzipan fruits, page 41, stages 7–10.

c) tiny choux buns or éclairs, page 67. Fill with butter icing, rather than cream, and shorten the baking time to about 10 minutes.

d) very small meringues, in various flavourings, see page 75 and below. These need not be sandwiched together.

e) small brandy snaps, as page 74, and the recipes on page 77.

Flavourings for meringues

Flavour the egg whites with a few drops of vanilla, almond or other essence. Do this sparingly; the flavour should be very mild. Blend 1 teaspoon sieved cocoa, or $\frac{1}{2}$–$\frac{3}{4}$ teaspoon instant coffee powder, with each 2 oz. sugar.

Nut meringues

2 egg whites
4 oz. castor sugar

2 oz. finely chopped hazelnuts or almonds (unblanched if wished)

Make the meringues as page 75, add the nuts *with* the sugar. Bake and use as meringues.

To crystallise petals

1 oz. gum arabic
2 oz. triple-strength rose water

flower petals, see method
castor sugar

Put the gum arabic into a dish and cover with the rose water. This is important so that you soften and dissolve the gum arabic well before use. (Buy from a chemist.)

Select the flower petals. They must be fresh and should never be picked after rain. IT IS DANGEROUS TO USE FLOWER PETALS FROM ANY BULBS, FOR MOST OF THESE CAN BE HARMFUL. The most useful and pleasant to look at are: rose petals, violet petals (or use the whole flower head), primrose petals and any flowers from the primula family, such as polyanthus. Fruit blossoms crystallise well, but are inclined to be very pale, but the flowering cherry, which often is a deeper pink, is a very good choice. Heather flowers look most attractive.

Hold the flowers by the stem or, if using individual rose petals, hold by the base. It is however, a good idea to pull off the very large rose petals and keep the smaller ones on the stem if possible. Paint the petals on both sides with the gum arabic and rose water mixture. Do this with a very fine paint brush. This must be done thoroughly otherwise they will not keep. Sprinkle carefully and thoroughly with castor sugar. Make sure both sides of the flowers are coated. Allow to dry. This can be done on trays, padded with kitchen paper, in really hot sun or in the oven after cooking, with the heat turned off, or in a warm airing cupboard.

When the petals are really dry, store in jars or tins. They keep for months.

To give a deeper colour you could add 1–2 drops culinary colourings to the gum arabic solution, but this makes the colour run when the petals are placed on to damp icing.

Use the petals on small cakes, petits-fours, desserts, etc.

To colour almonds

Put a few drops colouring on a plate, add the blanched nuts, turn in the colouring, allow to dry before using.

Almond petits-fours

	to glaze
oz. ground almonds	1 egg white
oz. castor sugar	
oz. sieved icing sugar	
ttle almond essence	**decorations**
egg	crystallised petals
ew drops sherry, brandy or	nuts
rum	cherries

Mix together the ground almonds, sugars, almond essence and the egg. (If making marzipan to ice a cake take some of this and work in the egg white to make a softer dough.) Add enough sherry, brandy or rum to flavour. The marzipan mixture must be sufficiently soft to pipe, it is best to moisten this with extra egg white, rather than liquid, as the mixture holds its shape better. Put a $\frac{1}{4}-\frac{1}{2}$-inch pipe into an icing bag, then put in the mixture. Force into shapes on a lightly greased baking tin or sheet. Brush with lightly beaten egg white. Bake for about 8–10 minutes in the centre of a moderate oven, 375 °F., Gas Mark 4–5, until very pale golden brown. Remove from the oven and press the decorations into the shapes while they are still soft. Allow to harden, store in an airtight tin. Makes about 30. These keep well, but become less moist after several weeks.

Macaroons

	decoration
egg whites	glacé cherries
ew drops almond essence	blanched almonds
–6 oz. castor sugar	
oz. ground almonds	
ce paper	

Whisk the egg whites and essence lightly. Add sugar and ground almonds. If the egg whites are large, use a little extra ground almonds to roll into balls. If piping the mixture, it may need softening with a little more egg white. Form into balls: for petits-fours the size of a hazelnut; for an ordinary biscuit about $1\frac{1}{2}$–2 inches; or pipe into fingers on rice paper on a greased in. Decorate with cherries and nuts. Bake for 2 minutes for small macaroons, or 20–25 minutes for the larger size, in the centre of a moderate oven, 350–375 °F., Gas Mark 4–5. Cool on tin, then cut round paper.

If you like a sticky macaroon, put a dish of water in the oven while cooking. Store in a tin, but eat within 2 days. Makes 12 biscuit size or 8 smaller size.

Chocolate finger macaroons

Make the macaroons as the recipe on the left. There is no need to put rice paper under the mixture on the tin, simply pipe on to the greased tin. Lift off when cold, and dip either end of the biscuits in melted chocolate, see page 43, stage 1, for details on melting this.

If preferred, sandwich two biscuits together with chocolate butter icing, page 13, and then dip the ends in the melted chocolate.

Macaroon gâteau

Make an almond-flavoured Victoria sandwich, page 16, or an almond-flavoured sponge, page 26. Do not add too much almond essence to the cake, a few drops will be enough. Sandwich together with whipped cream, to which is added chopped blanched almonds and a little sugar. Spread the whipped cream around the sides and on top of the cake, and press finger-shaped macaroons against the cake. Decorate with piped whipped cream between the macaroons. The biscuits should be added to the cake just before serving.

Meringues can be used in exactly the same way.

Florentines

4 oz. butter, poor weight	1 egg or 2 good
4 oz. castor sugar	tablespoons thick cream
3 oz. chopped almonds	
2 oz. flaked almonds	**decoration**
1 oz. candied peel	4 oz. chocolate, see page
1 oz. glacé cherries	69 for details

Melt the butter with the sugar in a pan, remove from heat, add almonds, chopped peel and chopped cherries. Cool, add the egg or cream. Mix well and put teaspoons of the mixture on well greased trays, allowing room to spread. Bake for 5 minutes in the centre of a moderate oven, 350–375 °F., Gas Mark 4–5, then look at the biscuits; if spreading too much pull the edges towards the centre with a palette knife. Continue cooking for a further 10–15 minutes, until golden coloured. Lift off tins, cool, coat one side with melted chocolate, page 43. These keep some days in a tin.

Your Questions Answered

I have many questions about icing, and I hope these points will help you if you have any problems when decorating cakes, etc.

Q. *What is the best way to tint icings, cakes, etc. ?*
A. Buy the best quality kitchen (culinary) colourings possible. Be sparing when using them. It is advisable to insert a skewer into the bottle and let a few drops fall from the skewer into the mixture. Remember that colourings are lost slightly when the mixture is baked in a cake, but that they remain in icings. For chocolate or brown colourings use a very little sieved cocoa.

Q. *Why is Royal icing sometimes a bad colour?*
A. This could be due to insufficient beating: while it is important not to over-beat and so incorporate too *much* air, you should beat until the icing is white. Some people like to add a drop of blue colouring. The other reason for a bad colour in Royal icing is that oil from the cake or marzipan can 'seep' through. See pages 38–41 about using marzipan, and coating the cake, and pages 44 and 45 about Royal icing.

Q. *Are there any icings that do not need boiling or icing sugar?*
A. Yes, the Marshmallow frosting on page 74. This is put on biscuits, but the same quantity is enough for a generous topping on a 7–8-inch sponge cake.

A *Jam Frosting* or *Jelly Frosting* is even easier. Melt a good tablespoon sieved jam or jelly; whisk an egg white, and gradually pour the warm jam or jelly on to the egg white, whisking hard as you do so. The frosting lasts on the cake (as would the Marshmallow frosting) for 2–3 days, but it is not successful to keep it in a basin, for after this time it would lose its shine if handled again. These frostings also make excellent fillings.

Q. *Why does a chocolate icing often lose its shine?*
A. It does of course depend upon the icing a chocolate butter icing will not have a shine a chocolate glacé icing has not a very high gloss. The best icing to use is just melted chocolate itself, see page 43, stage 1, or the melted chocolate icing on page 67. Both of these should have a good gloss. It is essential that chocolate is not over-heated during melting and the small quantity of oil or butter helps to retain the gloss.

Q. *How does one become good at neat even piping on a cake?*
A. First, practise handling icing pipes, etc. It is a good idea to use creamed potato when not making icing, and work out designs with this. Always plan the design beforehand, page 48 discusses this. Make sure the icing is the right consistency; if too hard, you cannot obtain an even flow and a smooth result; if too soft, the icing is easy to handle, but does not hold its shape. Read the details under the 'piping icings'; butter icing, page 13, and Royal icing page 44.

Q. *How does one get a flat coating on a cake that has risen too much?*
A. Either cut a slice from the top of the cake or turn the cake upside down and make the rounded part the base. If two sandwich cakes have both risen, then you can use the rounded tops as the centre part and make the filling so that it gives an even layer.

Marzipan can also be used to 'build-up' the edges of the top, until they are level with the risen centre. Most rich fruit cakes use plain flour to prevent their rising too much in the centre, see the comments, too, in the method for the Rich Christmas cake, page 46. Sponge cakes should be sufficiently moist to prevent their rising into a 'peak' in the centre.

Index

The following list gives the capacity of the U.S. standard measures and some ingredients in Imperial measures with American equivalents.

MEASURES

Imperial	American
1 teaspoon	1 teaspoon
1 tablespoon	1 tablespoon
$1\frac{1}{2}$ tablespoons	2 tablespoons
2 tablespoons	3 tablespoons
3 tablespoons	scant $\frac{1}{4}$ cup
4 tablespoons	5 tablespoons ($\frac{1}{3}$ cup)
5 tablespoons	6 tablespoons
$5\frac{1}{2}$ tablespoons	7 tablespoons
6 tablespoons (scant $\frac{1}{4}$ pint)	$\frac{1}{2}$ cup
$\frac{1}{4}$ pint	$\frac{2}{3}$ cup
scant $\frac{1}{2}$ pint	1 cup (8 fluid ounces)
$\frac{1}{2}$ pint (10 fluid ounces)	$1\frac{1}{4}$ cups
$\frac{3}{4}$ pint (15 fluid ounces)	scant 2 cups
generous $\frac{3}{4}$ pint (16 fluid ounces)	2 cups (1 pint)
1 pint (20 fluid ounces)	$2\frac{1}{2}$ cups

flour – plain or self-raising:

Imperial	American
	flour – all-purpose:
$\frac{1}{2}$ ounce	2 tablespoons
4 ounces	1 cup

cornflour: | **cornstarch:**

Imperial	American
1 ounce	$\frac{1}{4}$ cup
generous 2 ounces	$\frac{1}{2}$ cup
$4\frac{1}{2}$ ounces	1 cup

sugar – castor or granulated: | **sugar – granulated:**

Imperial	American
1 ounce	2 tablespoons
4 ounces	$\frac{1}{2}$ cup
$7\frac{1}{2}$ ounces	1 cup

sifted icing sugar: | **sifted confectioners' sugar:**

Imperial	American
1 ounce	$\frac{1}{4}$ cup
$4\frac{1}{2}$ ounces	1 cup

sugar – soft brown: | **brown sugar – light and dark:**

Imperial	American
1 ounce	2 tablespoons (firmly packed)
4 ounces	$\frac{1}{2}$ cup (firmly packed)
8 ounces	1 cup (firmly packed)

butter, margarine, cooking fat: | **butter, margarine, shortening:**

Imperial	American
1 ounce	2 tablespoons
8 ounces	1 cup

preserves: | **preserves:**

Imperial	American
12 ounces clear honey, golden syrup, molasses, black treacle:	1 cup (1 lb = $1\frac{1}{3}$ cups)
11 ounces corn, maple syrup	1 cup
5–6 ounces jam, jelly, marmalade	$\frac{1}{2}$ cup

dried fruit and nuts: | **dried fruit and nuts:**

Imperial	American
5–6 ounces raisins, currants, sultanas, chopped candied peel	1 cup raisins, currants, seedless white raisins, mixed chopped candied citrus peel
8 ounces glacé cherries	1 cup candied cherries
4 ounces halved shelled walnuts	1 cup
4 ounces chopped nuts (most kinds)	1 cup
3 ounces desiccated coconut	1 cup shredded coconut

miscellaneous: | **miscellaneous:**

Imperial	American
$\frac{1}{4}$ ounce gelatine	1 envelope gelatin